Some Sonnets

by Tom Matkin

Author's Note

This volume includes pretty much all the sonnets that I have written in the past 10 years or so, except for my Book of Mormon sonnet which I am publishing separately. That lifting of Book of Mormon sonnets out of the chronological flow accounts for why the sonnet numbers go out of whack as you read along. The gaps are filled in with Book of Mormon sonnets published elsewhere.

This book does include the sonnets that I wrote in 2009 as reflections upon the particular scriptures that were assigned to members of the Cardston Alberta Stake by the Stake Presidency as memorization scriptures.[i] The reader will want to have his or her scriptures at hand to fully appreciate "reflection" sonnets.

The "chapter" headings in this book are simply the year in which the poems were written. This is largely of no importance, but should help the reader better understand some poems which reference events going on at the time the poem was written. For example the writer made a visit to Nauvoo and Independence in 2001 and was moved to write poems about that and also the dedication of the Nauvoo temple in 2002. Some of these and other sorts of contextual matters are also explained in the twelve endnotes that are linked throughout and found on four pages following the sonnets.

Sometimes when it appears that not much was written in a particular year it is because I was focused on my Book of Mormon project at that time. Other times I was (hopefully) gathering strength for the future.

2001

Sonnet 1

The watermelon king dropped by tonight
A perfect match for those who cook by grill
So cool, sweet and colorful and light
Inviting everyone to have their fill.

And also came that queen, the cantaloupe
Quite equal to the king in taste and scent
Although a little less in size and hope
A fav of those who cater in a tent.

And scattered in the crowd from noon to dusk
Unroyal, minions of the melon set
These three, casaba, honeydew and musk
Maintained a lower humble silhouette.

The king, the queen, and courtiers on display
All hail to melons on a summer day!

Sonnet 2

These canyon walls are made of steel and glass
And concrete, stone, and bricks and bits of brass
And in the bottom of this civic glare
Are pavement rivers running everywhere.

No canyon here is ever boxed or blind
Because each one is carefully designed
Here nature's random hand is tamed and held
And every force and resource is compelled

To heed the greater need of man's control
With every part in service of this whole.
And workers, thick as ants, declare this place
A sign of progress for the human race.

Enough like this were lost, but now exhumed
To tell me that this city too is doomed.

Sonnet 3

When setting tile and filling in the grout
To wipe away each extra grain of sand
And clean inevitable messes out
I always keep a dampish rag on hand

I've found that there is need to be in haste
To clean the imperfections that adhere
Lest they should set and ever after waste
By showing smudges where it should be clear

Because when working in the dust and glue
There is no end to ways the sticky stuff
Can build up on the tiles and on you
And make what you want smooth back into rough.

The only hope for me to keep my tiling nice
Is in this good advice: Slop once. Clean twice.

Sonnet 4

The stoutest rope is only bits of string
Thus woven, piece by piece, to something great
And like it precious stolen moments bring
Strong cords to lift us from the hand of fate.

Short minutes stolen every single day
From out the things we think we need to do
Will bless us as we better learn to pray
And earn new skills as months and years accrue.

The power of the little done a lot
Is overlooked and oft misunderstood
And so we let these chances come to naught
And lose our opportunities for good.

And little bits of evil too can bind
As sins repeated seal the heart and mind.

Sonnet 5

We watch the clock in practiced wonderment
And track the progress of eternity
While grasping only shadows of the rent
That opens up the veil a faint degree.

Most travelers on this journey will not guess
That we are watching, timing, every move
Prepared to offer what we have to bless
And stage their opportunity to prove.

And so as they ascend to sacred heights
We calculate and concentrate our way
So we may join in time for these delights
That symbolize and seal a greater day.

This endless, timeless, everlasting walk
Ironically is ruled by a clock.

Sonnet 6

These simple words are all I know to write
So easy to pretend we understand
These words that soar then tumble like a kite
The victims of a weak or shortened strand.

A single word can never be quite true
It may be close, but in some way it's wrong
And weary explanations just won't do
The word is always still; too weak, too strong

Too off the mark, too kind, too sharp.
Still choose your every word with gentle care
And pluck them like an player at his harp
That they together may enrich the air

And harmonize those stark and single flaws
Into a chord that's true to one great cause.

Sonnet 7

When Andy backed into my rusty car
And crumpled up the door into a knot
I was standing in a temple not too far
Away from that ill fated parking spot

But after Missy's wedding was complete
And we exchanged the kisses and the hugs
I found that where my car had had a seat
Looked like it'd lost a battle with some thugs

But Andy left my neighbour a short note
I studied his impatient youthful scrawl
To figure what it was that he had wrote...
It said, what he had done, and would I call.

To learn your car is wrecked is really sad
Unless it proves a boy's an honest lad.

Sonnet 8

Along most any common roadside ditch
Are treasures for the senses and the heart
And though we fail to note the place as rich
Beyond intent it serves that better part.

We fly along the highway without thought
Oblivious to millions of details
And ever miss those things we have not sought
That frequent all these borders of our trails.

A wild rose may stretch her lovely head
Above the grass, then bow it back again
And note that in her busy flower bed
Some larks, and bees and foxes make their den.

We may not have the time to stop and stare
But still, I hope, we sometimes pause to care.

Sonnet 9

Far colder than a winter night is scorn
And even more to fear than ice, neglect
And windy blasts are never as forlorn
As glances which communicate reject.

Far sharper than a knife are evil cuts
Delivered by a tongue betraying trust
And worse than opportunity that shuts
Are portions measured with a scale unjust.

Yet greater even than these wrongs displayed
And far above the pow'r of cold or worlds
Is kind and tender mercy on parade
With flags of peace and charity unfurled.

Take faith. The tempered strength of love and right
Will always conquer evil's iron might.

Sonnet 10

When something heavy weighs upon your mind
And bothers every breath and thought and sense
It still may be too difficult to find
Articulation for its recompense.

These deeper wounds and sullen damning ways
May be too harsh, too sharp, too strong to bear
And so you suffer, minutes..., hours..., days!
Because you dare not face your hidden care.

Why can't you lay it all to simple guilt?
That enemy of peace for honest men,
What forces you to search a patchwork quilt
And brood for hours like a setting hen?

Rise up, attack the source of this torment.
Rise up. Rise up. Admit your guilt. Repent!

Sonnet 11

It seems one time may be a simple fluke
The chances are it will not come again
A random episodical rebuke
As far as anyone can ascertain.

But if perchance another comes your way
The odds that yet some more will come grow high
So you can bet, that from that fateful day
More painful incidents are drawing nigh.

I mark the day as August sixth this year
While I was on vacation at the 'Springs
That I was visited the second tier
With all the pain and suffering it brings.

So now I wait, a prisoner of fate,
Will my next kidney stone come soon, or late?

Sonnet 12

I've made the solemn call for civil talk
I've joined in the cry for tenderness
I've learned to love the mild and gentle walk
And kept my peace, unless I spoke to bless.

I've suffered slights and rudeness with a smile
I've shown patient happy diffidence
When faced with threats of unrestricted guile
I've turned the other cheek and moved off hence.

Yet just today I made a thoughtful note
Twas 'gainst the habit of the kind and meek
Instead it was quite harsh, the thing I wrote
The sort of thing I'm always loath to speak.

For just as Christ had need to cleanse His house
Sometimes one cannot play the timid mouse.

Sonnet 13

I thought how as the church was dear to me
The study of its origin and growth
And other aspects of its history
Would add something to covenants and oath.

And right I was as I began the quest
To learn of Joseph Smith and Brigham Young
I found and understood they were the best
Examples of the heart and mind and tongue.

Then someone said that history discussed
On-line upon another email list
Might add some life and take away the dust
So I subscribed to LDS and Hist.

Surprise, those fellows seldom get it right
It seems their only need, to find some blight.

Sonnet 14

Let's plan a lovely Paris day... We'll say,
A visit to the Louvre for most the time
Then dinner in a typical cafe
And "Carmen" at the Opera at nine.

We'll hope to see some history and art
The worthy kind that transcends time and space
And build and purify a willing heart
By basking in the glories of the place.

We will not take that friend who sees but wrong
Who points out the dust on picture frames
Whose seat's so hard he barely hears a song
And hates that food with funny Frenchy names.

Such friends have looked beyond the mark and missed
Until, at last, for them, no marks exist.

Sonnet 15

A question posed is wisdom's waking breath
Applying principles to every test,
Why must so much of life so presage death,
And how to from these wrongs the beauty wrest?

I doubt these eyes were given to stay blind
To anger, death, and evil or to lust
For if they focus on the One maligned
They'll find Him living not in peace and trust.

His scene the harvest of that sacred tree
That gives us choice because of what is known
And if we seek the light that helps us see
Then every opposite is clearly shown.

The fruit awakened us to evil rife.
The joy! And the burden, of this life.

Sonnet 16 (August 2001)

I have to have a browser that's robust
That has a lot of bells and whistles so
That when I need to print, or load or thrust
It simply takes me where I want to go.

And most of all it has to stable be
I can't be crashing every time I click
Illegal functions plague and worry me
This symptom of software whose code is sick.

Still when the browser asks for extra time
To think upon each question or demand
It makes me feel I'm wading 'round in slime
Instead of getting to the work at hand.

It's powerful, reliable, but slow
Is Netscape 6.1 the way to go?

Sonnet 17

It's time for me to move along, I guess
I'll go as swift and cool as a breeze
I hope you'll find I didn't leave a mess
I'll move along now quickly if you please.

It isn't that I want to go, you know
Or even that I feel you want me to
And I'm not really tired of this show
I'll miss it quite a bit... much more than you.

But something tells me I should move along
That there's another place and time for me
I hope I've left within your heart a song
To ease your mind and set your spirit free.

Somehow, its changed, and now I don't belong
You know it too. And staying would be wrong.

Sonnet 18

When duty's call requires my time the most
And leaves for light and happy solace naught
Thus is my soul with sterile time engrossed
And steals my heart by stony steely thought.

Above the pile the work may seem so small
And careless steps will take unmeasured toll
All that I build and organize will fall
Except the tasks that magnify my soul.

And yet to turn and gather only flowers
And fill your bosom but with cheer and love
Denies the need to exercise all powers
And clouds approving views from up above.

It's not enough to see the need for both
All duty, and all pleasure, I must loath.

Sonnet 19

Tis reason points the weary traveler home
And rescues him from grip of heartless strife
For each and every one who's wont to roam
Some harbour point gives logic to his life.

To drink again from fountains of our youth
To freshen what's depleted of our hope
And fill new reservoirs of strength and truth
We willfully return, so we can cope.

And these are yearnings not just of the mind
They echo through the soul and in the heart
Emotion also dictates that we find
Renewals of our spirit and our art.

Don't minimize or cast aside this need
You must step back before you can proceed.

Sonnet 20

Did you take notice of the crackling fire?
Of how it snapped and whooshed and popped and blew
A greedy grasping groaning gruesome pyre
Consuming what we held as good and true.

We teased it with our vain and foolish hope
And only fanned the flames much higher still
As eerie dancing demons claims each slope
Destroying the proudest forest hill.

But though it yielded not to fierce attack
And swallowed up our mightiest of blows
We crept around and probed it at its back
Where any fire's dying ember glows

And using patient steady stalking ways
We quenched the very bosom of the blaze.

Sonnet 21

The lessons learned in bitter heat and scorn
Are seldom ones that make a brighter day
But leave the learner lessened as he'll mourn
For what the condemnation took away.

Diminished, hurt and grieving from the blast
Some even lose the courage to forgive
And so the ugly scars that these wounds cast
Outlast, out wait, and finally, outlive.

Yet like the iron tempered into steel
By bitter heat and chilling scornful bath
Those chastened who can after learn to feel
True charity and nothing more of wrath

Shall stand in company of those most blest
And share in happiness above the rest.

Sonnet 22

A hundred sonnets neatly printed out
On paper fit to hand to any queen
And bound up in book that's true and stout
And written by a heart that's fine and clean.

A million roses thrust before my eyes
Each stripped of every defect, fault or thorn
In every ripened aspect, form or size
So perfect for the facets they adorn.

Or just as much as roses or a verse,
Some song, or mighty mountain, or a glen
Or sunset or a beach or scene diverse
May strike me with its beauty once again.

But all of these have lost their day and hour
Forever spoiled by your grace and power.

Sonnet 23

Forgotten wickedness from long ago
Despite the span of time may still be near
And though I hope its shadows do not show
This enemy may never disappear.

And though I cram and stuff its aspect deep
And think no more upon it day by day
And pile happy years upon the heap
I've only made more sure it's endless stay.

Nor can I slay or vanquish such a foe
I'm conquered if I set to conquer sin
I have to find a place for it to go
Then healing and redemption can begin.

The secret to the end of secrets known
Is only ever in atonement shown.

Sonnet 24

I rush from here to there and here again
Intent on duty, errands, plans and tasks
And sometimes stop, a pleasantry to feign,
Before resuming what my schedule asks.

I've studied all the ways to maximize
The management of motion and of time
I've sought to plot my life and synthesize
So everything I do is in the prime.

But every road and path that's on my way
Is occupied by someone with a need
And if I work my plan, I cannot stay
To comfort, soothe, console or bless, or feed.

Yet any kindness casts such magic charms
It sometimes works to heal a million harms.

Sonnet 25

Locked in the battle for my only heart
My foes are none but self and me alone
Tis I must choose, the worse or better part
And not some bitter enemy unknown.

I cannot offer blame for consequence
That's come from doings I have opted for
Tis by my will that I and decadence
Have reached this state of mutual rapport.

Still were I to have made a better end
Of this the product of my character
I should be prideful to, in fact, pretend
Twas I alone who was the whole factor.

If I give attribution for my good
Why is not likewise blaming understood?

Sonnet 26

No journey ever takes you anywhere
The scenery may shift but you remain
Unmoved, unchanged and always solitaire,
You are the essence of your own domain.

We think we come and go and travel far
We fool ourselves to such apparent truth
By measuring our motion by a star
Or in the time we age to sage from youth.

Still I pretend to take as fact these lies
And act as though there's really time and space
And wander happily between good-byes
And seek our separations to erase.

But just suppose that in the end it's true,
That you can't hie to Kolob. It's in you.

Sonnet 26

One day the dust was concrete, tough and strong
Magnificent, a glove to tempered steel
Designed to keep away most any wrong
Affixed, congealed, rock hard and truly real.

Then shaken by the force of evil wrath
What had been high, what had been solid stone,
Returned inevitably to the path
As weak and choking powder downward thrown.

Unfrocked, the girders twisted, fallen forms
Snake through the smoky dusty ruined heap
An awful, reckless grave that now performs
The ceremony where we go to weep.

The dust and ruined steel will soon be gone
But will the evil ever be withdrawn?

Sonnet 28

The big dogs shake their backs and scatter fleas
Annoyed by the bites of such small mites
But undeterred these dogs do as they please
They barely notice insects from such heights.

And all the while the smaller dogs and cats
Must show respect and favor for the great
And still they also suffer from attacks
From fleas and other minor things irate.

Oh they may wish the biggest dogs would aid
To snuff out all these pests that curse their lives
How many times these minor pets have prayed
For bigger dogs to unsheathe insect knives.

But then each little dog must fret in case
Some flea the big dogs seek hides in his place.

Sonnet 29 (My Best)

I'll wrestle with the worst that's part of me
To wrest unworthiness from out my soul
I'll test the truth against what I should be
Obsessed by that unreachable high goal.

Suggest another effort I should make
A quest with value measured on that scale
Detest the struggle that this fight will take
Protest the consequences if I fail.

I'll rest when only I can be assured
The guest that's in my heart is free from wrong
Possessed with confidence my spirit's cured
And blessed to lift an everlasting song.

The best I've ever done throughout this fight
Attests it can't be won with just my might.

Sonnet 30 (Fast Familiar Friends)

When fitful sleep and troubled anxious days
Entrap me in their cold and bony grasp
I search for hopeful, tender, happy ways
To loosen up their firm unwelcome clasp.

And as I study what's enlarged my woe
I often think it starts with what I want
And that because my satisfaction's low
The demons of desire are loosed to taunt.

Still honesty protests I'm not deprived
And all I'll ever need, and more, is mine
And so my nervousness is just contrived
A construct of my very own design.

Desire. Distress. Such fast familiar friends,
The hungry heart is where contentment ends.

Sonnet 31 (On the Shelf)

I could desire less and cure myself
From tattered rumpled dreams and wasted want
I could set my ambitions on the shelf
And hope they'd soon grow weak, infirm and gaunt.

With famine, self imposed, these troubling ghosts
Might leave me with a peace I've never known
As I through self control ignore their boasts
And neutralize the seeds that they have sown.

But even if by these denials planned
My happiness and joy's more assured
I have to wonder if my reach is banned
What greater price I'll pay for what's been cured.

The mis'ry of ambition's vain desire,
Or tragedy as precious dreams expire?

This Gracious Woman (Sonnet 32)

This gracious woman, beautiful and good
This gracious wife, affectionate and warm
This gracious lady, best of womanhood,
Disposed to tender kindness, and to charm.

This gracious mother, virtuous and strong,
Benevolent, and unafraid to pray,
Despising hate and hurt and painful wrong
Yet loving those who sin or slip or stray.

This gracious sister, humble, yet so right
So willing, happy, patient, suffering long
So elegant, yet modesty's delight,
A gracious angel blessing lives with song.

She knew the Savior, author of all grace,
And bore his loving image in her face.

The Devil Dances (Sonnet 33)

The devil dances in his special hell
Excited by the misery he's done
He shrieks a constant diabolic yell
It's what he's come to understand as fun.

The devil cannot ever be at rest
He's anxious, active, scheming, full of hate
And at his worst he's really at his best
Still mad because he lost his first estate.

He might be happy with the damage done
If happiness was something he could feel
But he's eternally destined to run
And satisfaction isn't in his deal.

Of course he has invited each to join
His fevered dance upon the red-hot coin.

Affection for Delay (Sonnet 34)

The thing I have to do will have to wait,
I'd rather do the things I want to do,
Besides. What does it matter if it's late
As long as it gets done before they sue?

Some people like to do their duty first
Before they ever think of fun or play
For me, I'm very happy I'm not cursed
To have no real affection for delay.

And every now and then a thing that was
Up high upon my list of things to do
Becomes, because of my habitual pause,
A thing I'm glad I never did pursue.

The early bird may keep his slimy worm
I'd sooner dine on meals long past their squirm.

Patience (Sonnet 35)

Why do we value patience in a man?
It seems a little contrary to me,
Just get it done as soon as soon you can!
That's pretty good advice. Don't you agree?

Why wait around for sober second thought?
You could be done before you think it through
And even if you're wrong at least you're not
Held up by analytical review.

So who's to say the patient man is wise?
His stock might just as easily go down
While he sits back and waits for it to rise
And ends up looking like a foolish clown.

I'm all for cutting once, I think that's nice,
But never ask this man to measure twice.

Modesty (Sonnet 36)

I like to have a counter on my site
And check in now and then to see the score
In dot com land, its hits, not right or might
That settles if you'll end up rich or poor.

In life, I think it's prob'bly quite the same
You can't be worth a lot unless the crowd
Comes frequently to check up on your game
And finds you captivating and quite loud.

I wonder if the decent, and the good,
The quiet, and the bashful, and the kind
Are hip to how they really prob'bly should
Behave and look a little less refined?

The squeaky wheel will usually get the grease
While modesty will get you stuck with peace.

Windy Rascal (Sonnet 37)

Ah time, that windy rascal, fresh and strong
When we take note of passage as a loss
We think, as youth, not of what now is gone
But what we gain from its capricious toss.

A moment here or there is like a year
To those who mark it as a thing to add
Tis as they might be caught, too young, for fear
They'll ever stay as just a lass or lad.

But when we feel that breeze begin to end
And like the wings of wisdom flown by
Time leaves off acting as our trusted friend
And drowns our desperate shouting with its sigh.

Deceived by time, it seems, from first to last,
I seek my timeless, everlasting past.

The Sonnet Nazi (Sonnet 38)

The sonnet Nazicame to visit me
No poem for you he gladly shouted out
And though he said it with a certain glee
I never paused to murmur or to pout.

Again he made his point with greater force
And threw his nasty chin up in the air
I simple stood and thought about the source
Then answered with my own resplendent flair;

Perhaps you think I need your silly gift
To write a simple sonnet quick as breath
I thought by now you'd start to get the drift
You have not pow'r to put my muse to death.

I'll write a sonnet anytime I please
And do it with extraordinary ease.

Looking for Leverage (Sonnet 39)

Veracity is heavy, strong and great
While every lie is airy, weak and slight
And that is why, to give falsehood some weight
It must be coupled with a grain of right.

And then to have effect of any sort
A marriage of deceit and rectitude
Will usually occupy some distant court
Far from the balance point of any feud.

When lightweight couplings try to pry this way
We often think to counter with our own
And thereby multiply our power play
Becoming oppositely overblown.

Not much of lasting peace or good, it seems,
Is done by those who advocate extremes.

The Fall (Sonnet 40)

The cool fall air defies the bright sun light
Reminding all that time is running out
With bright leaves spilling quickly, day and night,
Relentless in the calm or windy shout.

Afar the mountain tops are dusted white
And golden fields, undressed of any grain
Backdrop the sound of birds in restless flight
These migrants gathering above the plain.

But I shall never bend or change or move
Let seasons make their silly endless round
I'm unimpressed by what they have to prove
What can they say of where this creature's bound?

The winter night foreshadowed by this cold
Will earn no mention when my story's told.

The Cat's Paw (Sonnet 41)

The cat crouched down and reached his taloned paw
Towards his enemy ferociously
And blood was all that anybody saw
As he dispatched his foe so handily.

And then the cat resumed his masquerade
A dozing, quiet, friendly sort of chap
Who seemed to barely notice the parade
That wandered innocently by his trap.

Some say the cat, if he would be declawed,
Would be no further danger to the peace
But others guess this reasoning is flawed,
All cats must go! Before this blood will cease.

I study how my fingernails are cut
And feel a knot of worry in my gut.

Love Poems (Sonnet 42)

A verse of love should never mind the state
Of those whose hearts are met to make two one
Nor should debased pedestrian debate
Of status even enter in the fun.

One hopes, of course, that courtship once begun
Will end in holy wedlock every time
And that no couple's passions setting sun
Will hasten when their wedding bells will chime.

But still, perhaps, there's something more sublime
When each is bound by bands of vows of love
And that they make thereby an upward climb
To something worthy, better, and above.

The suitors makes a poem to seduce
The spouse, perhaps, for reason and excuse.

The Move (Sonnet 43)

The course we set was difficult, but good
To move among your people in your land
And leave my country and our neighborhood
Retirement meticulously planned.

It fell together marvelous and grand
A rush of choices, houses bought and sold
It seemed like providence's helping hand
Was on us as we watched our plan unfold.

But suddenly the whole thing just went cold
Your cough, and then your sickness, then your death
And everything we wanted or controlled
Has vanished like your final painful breath.

And here am I in strange and foreign place
Alone. And lost. In misery's embrace.

Night Vision (Sonnet 44)

I like to walk the hills and roads at night
To stretch myself along the blackened earth
And feel the starlight's penetrating might
And contemplate the force of death, and birth.

I like to shade my face from sunlight's burn
And stand in shadows deep and cool and dark
And take refreshment from a day's concern
Through lessons luminated by a spark.

Why seek for truth in brightly lighted ways
When simple contrast casts the finest points
And universes stand out in faint rays
Then disappear when light of day anoints?

For me, each subtle flash of night time fire
Exposes day time vision as the liar.

News! (Sonnet 45)

I struggle with obscure and ancient things
It took me years to see Isaiah's part
And curiosity about Ezekiel brings
No comfort to this modern stony heart.

I have no gift for Greek or Latin lore
And Hebrew grammar stupefies my mind
And Shakespeare barely penetrates my core
Antiquity is lost upon my kind.

And so I have to celebrate some news
Of something very fresh and avant garde
It's bound to liberate my faithful muse
And easy up for me what once was hard.

In just one month, (the word has just come down)
Shaw cable will bring broadband to our town!

CNN (Sonnet 46)

I'd like to see the end of CNN.
Go back to when Sports networks drew me in
I guess I mean back to September 10
Before I'd even heard of Laden Bin.

I like that guy I've met named Aaron Brown
His manner's perfect for this time and place
But I'll be happy when he's not around
And Ernie Johnson occupies my space.

It's not that anthrax scares me very much
Or even bombs and missiles in Afghan
It's just that all this terror is a touch
Too close to home for now and for this fan.

So just for now I'll stick with Larry King
And hope I'm back with Ernie by the spring.

Shopping at the Big Box (Sonnet 47)

Two men in rough wool hats and long dark coats
Slide through the door into the "big box" store
Behind them with their scarves tied 'round their throats
Are women. Dresses brushing 'long the floor.

They move together in a practiced way
The women always staying just behind
Though, evidently having much to say
The voices of this group, if not the mind.

My eyes and ears are curiously drawn
Towards this strange and foreign entourage
The chatter, not an unfamiliar song,
Reminds me nothing here is just mirage.

They sample pizza, soup and soda pop
Then buy some nuts and quickly leave the shop.

Intelligence (Sonnet 48)

I lay me down in deep and fluid grass
Below the brightest blue that ever was
Quite hidden from what ever comes to pass
Oblivious to what the world does.

I smell the fruitful earth along my back
And feel the unseen sun upon my face
And everything is blue and green, then black
Absorbing all of me without a trace.

Perhaps some thing a bit like DNA
Preserved before I ever made my cry
Awaits to show me back to light of day
Intelligence that doesn't ever die.

I search for such a theory to explain
How any man could ever live again.

Rest (Sonnet 49)

Relax my friend and take an easy look
Release your anxiousness and settle back
Remind yourself, it's not the time it took
Rejoice and savor momentary slack.

Extend yourself with quiet calming time
Erase the errors of your hasty life
Evade the folly of the social climb
Eschew whatever causes pain or strife.

Stay true to principles and kindly arts
Surrender to the voice that calls for peace
Select more carefully the better parts
Submitting to what may afford release.

Tomorrow may demand more than my best
Today, then, while I can, I'll take a rest.

Farewell L (Sonnet 50)[ii]

That ancient Roman numerologist
Forgot to figure numbers in his test
And using letters made a nasty twist
When math should be a much more simple quest

It's kinda hard to add a column when
No decimal points are obvious or true
Or when you get to forty and just then
You have to use an L for something too.

I fell into this trap with sonnetry
Devising how to keep a simple count
And now its worse than high geometry
To figure out every sonnet's next amount.

There's better ways to count, the truth to tell,
And so from Sonnet L, I bid farewell.

Balance (Sonnet 51)

I held my hands up high and called his name
Unsure if he might hear a simple call
And knowing if he didn't I would blame
Much timidness as leading to my fall.

No subtlety or grace or even pride
Could be allowed to cloud my need to know
And so I rudely, loudly, proudly cried
Against all nature's evil noisy flow.

But had I listened half as well I might
Have heard the answer to my hopeful cry
And if I'd looked more rightly at the light
I might have been contented with my try.

I pray for faith and patience and the scope
To balance my requests with silent hope.

Summer Breezes (Sonnet 52)

We easily withstand a summer breeze
In fact, it cools and fortifies the soul
It never. Never. Brings us to our knees
It plays a gentle comfortable role.

We feel much stronger by its mild kiss
The noon day sun seems less to be a foe
And nothing. Nothing. Ever seems amiss
While tender, easy, summer breezes blow.

But where I live much wind is not so kind
It gathers dust and fire and ice and cold
And standing up against its fickle mind
Demands a heart that's brave and strong and bold.

I'll take the solace summer breezes bring
While standing strong because of winds that sting.

Leave Your Message (Sonnet 53)

Annoyed by the telephone at night
I fixed the trouble with a simple thing
I'm not exactly certain that it's right
But I just go on sleeping through it's ring.

I've found that what a body can get done
In wee and dark and late late midnight hours
Is seldom very much and never fun
And always messes up my daylight powers.

Of course I leave my answering machine
To comfort those who try to call me late
Or I'll look at the i.d. caller screen
To see just who it is that I've made wait.

So if you've called me after I'm asleep
You'll have to leave your message at the beep.

Focus (Sonnet 54)

Why can't I get my focus narrowed down
To one or maybe only two concerns
Why must my mind be spread so much around
It seems to make no progress, only turns?

I worry here, then there, and then back here
I change my notions almost every week
I vacillate from comfort, then to fear
And race from misery to cheery peak.

At least I'm not just at one thing too much
I never seem to dig a rut too deep
Or lose the luck beginners like to touch
Or stumble into burn-out's foolish creep.

I wonder if my busy shallow ways
Are permanent, or just another phase?

A Shadow (Sonnet 55)

A shadow crossed his eyes and killed his smile
As he recalled, again, just what she'd said
He'd kept it out of mind for just a while
Now one more time, false hopes were lost to dread.

Forgetful as he was of many things
It bothered him that this commanded place
And that the comfort loss of memory brings
Was now, too fleeting in its cold embrace.

To bear the visit of this loathsome news
Intruding on his body, mind and soul
Demanding of him that he caref'lly choose
What parts to guard as he gives up the whole.

He hopes that when what's vuln'rable is gone
There's still enough that's left to carry on.

Enos, The Hunter (Sonnet 56)

I never venture out without my phone
I have no love for solitary creed
And being in the wilderness alone
Has never been a passion or a need.

Still Enos seems to grab some part of me
When he describes his wrestle in the sticks
And how he managed to become sin free
By mighty prayer out far from roads and bricks.

Could this mean that I'm wrong to spurn the wild
And that I ought take the firearm's course
Now offered for each hunter, man and child
And thereby gain communion with my Source?

I hope that we can taste that special feast
Without the need to hunt the wild beast.

Shudda Been a Limerick (Sonnet 57)

What part of chicken dinner is the best?
I don't mean gravy, veggies or the soup
I'm talkin' about the leg, the thigh, the breast....
Yes, what's the best of what comes from the coop?

I'll state my case for what I care for most,
The simple chicken leg would top my list
So succulent and tasty, it's the toast
Of those who upon flavour do insist.

The breast is far too dry and gags me up
And while I like the thigh I have to say
It's messy if I hold it while I sup,
And don't put backs or wings on my buffet.

Yes what delight could ever hold a candle
To food that comes complete with it's own handle?

Common (Sonnet 58)

I seek to make my peace with God alone
Not giving up to man my choice or way
I know sometime I'll kneel before His throne
And want to be found worthy on that day.

So pious, penitent and holy things
Are foremost in my thoughts and frequent prayers
I want to know the peace devotion brings
And not give thought to common earthly cares.

But He whose life and death demands my eye
Concerned himself with service to the poor
He taught the doctrines which condemn the high
And healed and blessed and lived with the obscure.

I have to be above each common sin
Yet serve among the common folk like Him.

Sonnet 59 (Tragedy)

A tiny blip upon my radar screen.
Somewhere, I note, a tragedy takes place
But still I rarely vary my routine
And soon the blip is gone without a trace.

I s'ppose it ever has been just this way
We learn so little from a sudden fright
Resolve born of an instant will not stay,
It sparks. Then vanishes into the night.

Still now and then, disaster, for its size,
Or closeness, or some other fearful thing
Will turn my heart and help me empathize
With sorrows that calamities can bring.

But really, don't I always draw a line
Between your grief and what I see as mine?

Sonnet 60 (Almost)

It's almost more than any man can take
These hours in the saddle and the sun
Where wicked windstorms stir me to my break
And rain and sleet and muddy rivers run.

Where angry clouds provide the only roof,
A scant and mean and faithless covering,
And every day and night there's bitter proof
That something worse is nearby hovering.

Oh yes, at dawn my heart may gather hope
Of brighter, clearer, kinder, tender times
Or even now against a purple slope
A blood red sunset seems to sing in rhymes.

So terrible, yet beautiful, this ache
It's almost more than any man can take.

Sonnet 61 (Shell)

The poisoned dart that fills my heart with pain
Was cast with reckless carelessness and at
Someone so dear, someone so near, the stain
That marked her harm, marked me as well as that.

Perhaps as much as any touch on her
While not directed at, has wounded me.
And we can't be again the way we were
Though others may not know or ever see.

My wounded heart may heal, in part, in time
And glad and happy days replace my gloom
But tender bonds as love responds sublime
Decree that we will share each others gloom.

I dare not build a shell to shield my soul
For fear the shell might stand between our whole.

Sonnet 62 (Sparks)

The man who strikes a spark with flint and steel
And drops it into tinder from his hand
May have a sense of fire's bright ideal
And think the flame will spread just as he planned.

He probably has some kindling and some sticks
And even wood piled high behind his house
And maybe has a fireplace of bricks
And figures when his needs are met, he'll douse.

But once a spark has flamed into a fire
It doesn't always burn as one may like
It meets, exceeds or fails that man's desire
And sometimes he regrets he made the strike.

I wonder if the notions that make verse
Behave a little like the sparks... or worse?

Sonnet 63 (Patience)

I think the patient, prudent man is dull
He cannot have the sharpened edge that's best
To cut into the flesh of life that's full
Of tantalizing, captivating zest.

How can he be enthused with what he does
If he controls his passions all the time
If he's content with who and what he was
How can he force a constant upward climb?

Still always there's the danger that the zeal
Of those who cast off patience as a weight
Will too soon burn the fuel that would seal
A happy, long term, satisfact'ry state.

I think someday I'll make my patience grow
Till then, I'll patiently detest what's slow.

Sonnet 64 (Gaps)

We weave a web of fantasy between
The rare and simple things we really know
Our guess of what is real but still unseen
We try to demonstrate with things that show.

And these embodied notions quite untrue
May make a picture that deceives the eye
Until our simple minds believe what grew
From what might plainly, sadly, be a lie.

Some fill the space between the anchoring points
With faith, while others rather live in doubt.
Like long and sturdy bones between the joints
What's in these gaps is what it's all about.

I hope as I connect from dot to dot
I'm proven right more often than I'm not.

Sonnet 65 (Moods)

I wonder who's in charge of setting moods,
Of giving me perspective, bright or dim,
Whose job is it to see my day includes
An attitude that's positive, or grim?

I wonder if a guardian of sorts
An angel, or a spirit, is assigned
To lift me or to bury me in torts,
To settle if my day is mean or kind?

Sometimes I guess it's only up to me
No other person has the pow'r or right
To set the mood for how and what I'll be
To keep me focused on the dark, or light.

Still other times I'm sure I had no say
In just how low I seem to feel that day.

Sonnet 66 (Polishing)

Some shining things won't ever meet the eye
Unless they're worked and coaxed up from below
We have to rub and polishes apply
Before the golden fire will ever show.

Removing dross and smudging particles
And adding what may magnify the light
Requires effort mixed with articles
Of faith to make the dark give way to bright.

Still, even if we fail to do the task
And leave the gems and jewels in their gloom
The shining thing is still behind that mask
Disguised in an ephemeral costume.

I want to learn and exercise the craft
Of manufacturing the polished shaft.

Sonnet 67 (Types)

Perhaps you only see a rock. Or bread.
Or when you touch the rain or feel the snow
Or plunge your feet into a river bed
You're only feeling water in the flow.

Perhaps you even think that Ammon's quest
Was just his own adventure, nothing more,
Or sacrificing Isaac was a test
For only Abraham, in times of yore.

But if you think of these as shadows of,
Or types or symbols of the Living Christ
You'll have a greater taste of heaven's love
And see in everything atonement priced.

All things bespeak of Father and the Son
And of the need to let our hearts be won.

Sonnet 68 (New Dell)

I see okay when looking in a pinch
My eyes aren't really weak or bad as yet
But still I like my screen that's nineteen inch
And love my mother board to be a jet.

My hearing isn't bad, it's really good
And I can't tell a woofer, sub from par,
So maybe I just bought this cuz I could
My mid life toy, like a red sports car.

Well then again it might be that my job
Requires me to have a DVD
And I'm not being bad or like a snob
To run a Pentium Four and Write CD.

And having XP Pro and is really swell
For writing sonnets on my brand new Dell.

Sonnet 69 (Understanding)

I think we have a notion that we know
Each other, in a hopeful, useful, way
And we will often let this notion show
In how we get along from day to day.

And science ever tries to understand
The roots of interactions between men,
The categories endlessly expand
Of different social studies and their ken.

And yet it seems our understanding's less
For all the science we apply to this
Society stays in its hopeless mess
And always, peaceful theories go amiss.

Perhaps the key to understanding man
Is only found in learning heaven's plan.

Sonnet 70 (Satan's Girlfriend)

Her verse seems stuck in just one place and time
One note, monotonous, and monotone,
No variation in the hope or rhyme
Cold written words no friendlier than stone.

Her name is borrowed from the fires of hell
A raging victim of her willingness
To yield herself to things too proud to tell
Enslaved by tragic fondness for excess.

No cunning words or crafty plans of men
Will ever serve to save this devil's child
No fallen mate can push or pull her when
Her wretched heart's so thoroughly beguiled.

But, if she will, she still may find that friend
Who'll rescue anyone from such an end.

Sonnet 71 (Tender)

Be kindly to the lost and lonely one
Be tender, tender, kind, and full of love.
It may be clear his faith has come undone
And you may feel to give his heart a shove.

But hold your quick and rough correcting hand
And use instead, with him, a touch that's mild
To gently help him want to understand
And feel the joy of truth as heaven's child.

Still it will always take a good deal more
Than common kindness, matched with friendship's arm
To lift a drowning sailor to the shore
And save him from deserved cruel harm.

But cold despair and chastening's not rare.
It's tender care, and fellowship that's spare.

Sonnet 72 (Illinois and Missouri)

These lands are far too free of any sign
Of people, living people, gathered round.
I cannot see them, yet there's in my spine,
A resonating, supernatural sound.

They came to stay. And built a mighty land.
And left their tears and blood and graves and hopes,
A righteous, anxious, over zealous band
Who ploughed and dressed and loved these fertile slopes.

Oh, mostly, they moved on to better times
And I have been an heir to what they did
And I should happily forget the crimes
That wrecked this reckless Zionistic bid.

But still, to visit, on these vacant fields
There is no telling what such suff'ring yields.

Sonnet 73 (Southern Wyoming)

No tree can grow in such a bitter place
The brutal winds that burrow every where
Destroy any seedlings chance for grace
And trade the faintest hope into despair.

It's only sage and rough and rugged brush
That set this land apart from distant moons
And summer's heat and winter's frigid rush
Make harsh and hostile Decembers and Junes.

Still there are hardy, hopeful, stoic folk
Who've made this stark and cruel state their home
While many others, passing through, may joke
It's only fit as somewhere from to roam.

I've never lived in such a place, it's true,
So I won't try to judge why others do.

Sonnet 74 (Nauvoo)

The fallen monarch combs neglected hair
Restoring beauty from a tangled mess
Preparing once again to show, and share,
Her dignity in all its loveliness.

Her face, long dimmed by enemies of state,
Is full of hope and faith and newly bright
And seems to suddenly forget the wait
This patient queen has had in lesser light.

There is no promise she will ever reign
As primal monarch of her subject ones
But she may take her honoured place again
As mother of unnumbered worthy sons.

At last, resplendent in her rightful gown,
She bows, and rev'rently accepts her crown.

2002

Sonnet 75 (Retro)

Some retrospective sorts like things of age
And find that looking back's a source of joy
They seem to value most the well read page
And fads and fashion from the past employ.

They speak most often of the good old days
And seldom think of how things are just now
For what is past they have unbridled praise
It's clear for them, what's old's the cat's meow.

Still others find the past a dreary note
For them the future's only where it's at
And idle talk of hist'ry gets their goat
It's boring, never radical or phat.

I think I understand both points of view
Because for me, the past is always new.

Sonnet 76 (Honour Bound)

The man whose treachery is honour bound
Who deems himself to be too awf'lly right
And patiently desires that he be crowned
Will will his many victims not to fight.

This man who coldly builds his army's might
And gathers fearful souls with death and pain
And loves the pow'r that power can ignite
Must, in the end, find his achievements vain.

Each ever faithful friend of good and right
Who with a perfect courage can be found
Who turns his heart instead from dark to light
Is thus more honestly called honour bound.

The best and worst of men each take a vow
To test which passions all the rest allow.

Sonnet 77 (Snags)

I snagged a single thread and broke it free
And where there had been texture, strength and shape
Unraveled now a frank apology
A rip, a rent, a tear, a weak escape.

The only single thread that one could see
Distinct from all the whole and intact ones
Was this thread ruined carelessly by me
Now sep'rate from a million woven sons.

We often mend, at least to some degree,
The snags and tears that shred our daily weave
And count this needed blessing in our plea
For what we hope and pray God will relieve.

What plagues me is how easily I rend
Compared to what it takes to make a mend.

Sonnet 78 (Dope)

Forget those simple joyful happy times
When life was good and fortune smiled on you
Erase the memory of those better climes
When sunshine beamed across the sparkling dew.

Don't dwell so much on how it used to be
You can't go back, your life is ever changed
It's torture when you think you once were free
And now you see how far from that you've ranged.

Oh sure, sometimes, you think a bit of hope
Is shining in the distant darkened sky
But hey there, don't be such a foolish dope
It's only taunting, teasing, you to try.

You know you forfeit every joy of man
The day you set to 'minister a LAN.

Sonnet 79 (Untried Wings)

I easily give up the thing that's tough
Deciding quickly that it's far too hard
Declaring soon that I have had enough
Retreating once again to my backyard.

I save myself the trouble of defeat
By sticking with the tried and true so well
To know, almost at once, when I've been beat
Saves me from fates of those who tried and fell.

Still lingers in my modest simple mind
The notion that perhaps much greater things
Someone who's just like me might haply find
By stretching inconvenient untried wings.

Shall I rest safely on familiar shore
Or shall I fly against the wind and soar.

Sonnet 80 (Dawn)

Casting long shadows the morning sun slipped
Between the trees, along the river's rim
Flashing in the leaves, sparkling as it tripped
Across the dancing waters of the swim.

And chasing off the shade of moonlit night
Replacing black and grey with colored day
Awakening the pow'rs of wholesome light
To signal birth of this, a better way.

I've slept beyond this moment countless times
And had no sense of missing dawn's delights
But in this instant all of nature's rhymes
Exploded as another day rewrites.

I hope before this daylight blinks good-bye
More beauty still will catch my weary eye.

Sonnet 80 (Quake on Hyde Street)

In Orson's borrowed room they huddled close
Too many for this tiny cabin space
But gathered thus they dared to each suppose
That God should bless them with His solemn grace.

All nine, in turn, would speak and pray as one
To know the will of heaven for this place
And once this counseling of men was done
They sought for God's demonstrative embrace.

The door was breached by neighbours in distress
"An earthquake shook our houses" so they cried.
Though ground had trembled at decision blessed
No quake was felt among the men inside.

Their witness, heard by each, and undenied
"Step forth my servant Brigham, and preside!"

Sonnet 82 (A Nod)

A wink, a nod, a smile, a gesture kind
A wave, a hug, a word of honest cheer
Just recognition by a friendly mind
That someone's pleased to see that someone's here.

The touch and clasp of gentle willing hands
Bestowing nothing more than frank respect
And nothing less than what each heart demands
Some simple proof of how we all connect.

Can these small trifles really have effect?
Far better to be warm with those we know
Than waste our good without a sure reflect
Upon mere strangers as they come and go.

So if I practice this benign neglect
How will this help my character perfect?

Sonnet 83 (Sudden Snow)

Sometimes the snow comes suddenly and we
Are caught, cold. Frozen in its violent clutch,
We think. Oh how much better it might be
If we weren't taken by surprise so much.

We have the Weather Channel and the news
We have our local knowledge of the sky
We have the way our bones behave to choose
If winter snow is coming soon, and why.

Of course we really always know it will
The very day and hour shouldn't care
We know each life encounters winter's chill
So why put off the things we should prepare?

And then, beyond the snow's a brighter day
Where fresh astonishments come into play.

Sonnet 84 (Costumes)

A tiny creature made for Halloween
So scarcely understanding what or why
This innocent so cute and so obscene
Confused, like us, if it should laugh or cry.

A dancer, born to feel the music's beat
Not sure what menace lurks in loving this
The tunes not ever true or truly sweet
Like loving less the lover than the kiss.

Some never guess the costume is the child
That no disguise is hiding what you are
And so a cloak you think has us beguiled
Is no more false than any other scar.

But everything is meant to make this clear
That things are never quite what they appear.

Sonnet 85 (Mixed)

I'll gather no more roses to my lips
I'll drink no more of beauty with my eyes
Nor let the rain run through my fingertips
Or ever think of singing with my thighs.

And I won't be persuaded by my tears
Or change the bitter worry in my hair
I can't be flattened by my daily fears
Or plant myself into a rocking chair.

My back is far too happy to be up
My head won't spin, nor will my heart be still
And how can I be hungry if I sup
Upon a feast of poems fit to kill.

One cannot get enough of metaphor
It's image laden speech that I adore.

Sonnet 86 (Toll)

I may have made a bargain for my soul
A trade whereby I gave and got a prize
I may still have to pay the final toll
And mark my deal as sorry and unwise.

I may not have been brave when it was right
To stand against injustice I have seen
And cowardly refused to stay and fight
When doing what was weak and small and mean.

But life still holds me to this dusty path
And while it does I'll count as done these sins
And hope to find a refuge from the wrath
That wicked foolish selfish living wins.

And needing what I've earned the least of all
I plead for grace to save me from my fall.

Sonnet 87 (Troll)

They lurked below the village bridge, I hear,
And bothered billy goats, I think, the most
They sought to victimize with fright and fear
Convincing innocents that they were toast.

It's said they mainly came in hues of green
(Could jealousy have been what spurred them on?)
But truthfully these things were never seen
So what they were can't really be foregone.

Though now we find a modern etroll sprite
That lurks on email lists and there abouts
Whose nasty snap and bark exceeds his bite
Who sells a mix of mockery and doubts.

Still one must give the virtual troll his due
Without him email traffic turns to glue.

Sonnet 88 (Blood)

What's in the blood to love the castanet
And join the thrill of proud and pounding feet,
Of bright and dark flamenco dancing set
To music driven by its primal beat?

What makes a heart respond to delta blues
Those songs lamenting every life's complaint
That mix the ugly and the lovely hues
With tension and resolving chords as paint?

What's in the soul embraces wild drums
Or cruel pipes or wailing native criers
Or settles with the harmony of strums
Upon guitars, sitars, or harps or lyres?

I hope that heaven takes our mixed up choir
And purifies the lot. With love... and fire.

Sonnet 89 (Cyclops)

There is no need to drive a hot sharp stick
into the giant's eye. Because I know
he is already as blind as a brick,
Though he wants me to think it isn't so.

But he cannot see, he can only lie
and probe for weaknesses in my armor.
So I'm not bothered by his single eye
He only glories for himself, I'm sure.

I shall not fear the giant's hopeless role
but rather fear my weakness as I try
to mend and build and make my armor whole
against the giant's blows, both low and high.

And, clinging to a lamb, I understand,
Will save me from the grasp of giant-land.

Sonnet 90 (Seminary Answers)

The seminary answers play across
The dull and narrow field that is my mind
Is this the way it is, or just a gloss?
There must be mysteries for me to find.

To study, pray, and work seems not enough
Too simple, not requiring very much
Such normal, easy, ordinary stuff,
Demanding nothing but the common touch.

But is it really ordinary fare
To master what is basic in the writ
Or understand profoundly about prayer
Or how to make a stony heart submit?

The mystery is how to win the fight,
And exercise the things we know are right.

Sonnet 91 (Sealed)

I could not count the colors in your eyes,
The worlds hidden in your happy heart
Nor could I understand the constant prize
That sets your glad and singing smile apart.

These portals to the infinite are mine!
And yours! We share them differently but true
And nothing else, for me, is quite so fine
As binding hope and love sealed up with you.

Our union is a seer stone, doubly blessed,
To comfort, hold and temper in this day
And promise greater that the earth can test
When mortal dross is finally burned away.

Invited in, and compassing as host
The Father and the Son and Holy Ghost.

Sonnet 92 (Tapioca)

Some tapioca lovers ride this train
And nuts who study languages and such
And some who never walk without a cane
And I saw one guy hobbling with a crutch.

And singers, quite a few, I'm sure on board
And several here with bicycles at home
And one I saw was carrying a sword
And there's a family here they call Jerome.

And even we have people with brown eyes
Though some are green and others blue as ice
And some wear coats and hats and fancy ties
While others find more casual wear is nice.

With all these different folks, how did they choose
To only search and take away the Jews?

Sonnet 93 (Reflections on Alma 13:21)

A simple gesture, reaching out to touch,
A stretch, a movement signaling to all,
That lifted hand that means so very much.
Powerful. Proof he's magnified his call.

A minister, a prophet and a seer
A brother, fellow elder and a priest
A judge and teacher trying to bend near
To those who seem to want his message least.

And then, the gesture giv'n, a mighty voice
The testimony of his faith rings out
Demands they make a soon and solemn choice
Condemns them for their sin and pride and doubt.

High priesthood reaching out to love. Then shake.
In hopes that hopeless sinners will awake.

Sonnet 94 (Remember)

This short delay between two worlds forgot
This spark between two great eternal flames
This life, too small, too large, too cold, too hot
This qualifying meet, between the games.

No angels seen will herald as you're born
Nor will the mountains tumble when you die
Your passage, a small page that's roughly torn
From out the endless book of life's supply.

Still, everyone who comes is known by name
By Him who paid in blood for every debt
And though we none are ever quite the same
We share the curse of what we each forget.

For you, dear child, I have but one desire,
Find memory in mysteries and fire.

Sonnet 95 (The Losing Battle)

The folks I used to know have now grown old
They struggle against gravity and time
Not crisp nor sharp nor quick nor even bold
Their power and their glory, past its prime.

The folks I knew back then were strong and bright
Untamed a bit, I guess, but full of hope
With promise, opportunity and light
They pushed and pressed and pulled to lift their scope.

And many that I knew with backs now bent
And prospects broken down by nature's toll
Have, while their flesh and bones were being spent,
Been building something greater in the soul.

And I believe we'll triumph if we choose
To fight this battle everyone must lose.

Sonnet 97 (My Marker)

I've walked between the tombstones many times
And entertained what marker suits me best
Should it display a few of my best rhymes
Or scales of justice, as a solemn crest?

Perhaps the names of children who were mine
Upon this earthly test, should be etched in
Or should the temple be emblazoned fine
To show the promises I hope to win?

But then I stop before one small and plain
A child's, decorated with a lamb
And see my marble notions as too vain
And ponder how to mark the great I Am.

Instead of planning tribute to my sleep
Perhaps I should be feeding hungry sheep.

Sonnet 96 (Reach Back)

Reach back beyond the distant harvest moon
Beyond the mists of memory gone cool
Much sooner that the harsher light of noon
Your dawning as a glad and simple fool.

It's time to find your happy self again
To strip away the scars that hide your flesh
Like armour keeping you from devil rain.
It's time. Reach back. Renew, revive, refresh.

Yes, dare to open up a past delight
To breach the ramparts built against the past
And leave unguarded doors long locked up tight
To seek to have sweet memories recast.

Don't say you'll yield yourself not now, but soon,
Already, it is late, late afternoon.

Sonnet 98 (Enticement)

Enticement and seduction. Calling out.
The siren, shrill and sweet, to take you in
It wants to make you know, to wish, to doubt
Like rivers on a rock destined to win.

It's patient and elastic in its quest
Chamaeleon and camouflage and cloak
This crack defines the granite of your test
And hangs around your fire like woodsmoke.

You flail against its tentacles in vain
To conquer you must more than contradict
Your legacy is bankruptcy and pain
Unless you turn your back to this conflict.

It isn't fighting sin defeats the foe
It's yielding to the other, better flow.

Sonnet 99 (Ice)

It's ice. So clean, so crisp and crystal hard
Reflecting light. Blinding, flashing, gleaming
Above a lake. Brilliant, stirring, scarred.
Black at its heart. Frigid vapors steaming.

A diamond in the day. Rifle shots of change
A mirror to the moon. A night of growing pains.
It's polished by snow, sifting, silent, strange.
Patient in this wind. Not nourished by its veins.

This crusty, scaly, quilted, blanket skin
Wrung out, too grim, too bleak, severe. Congealed.
This glacial upstart which can never win
Whose losing war with warm is sure, and sealed.

It's ice. And its cold promises cement
The truth, that even elements repent.

Sonnet C (See)

I wonder what a blind man really sees?
With darkened screen that's never washed with light
He cannot see the sunset or the trees
Is dim, for him, as equal as the bright?

He smells and feels and hears and learns quite well
The world that surrounds him day to day
But still, I wonder, since his eyes don't tell
If in his mind there's endless, formless grey?

Though as for me I sometimes see far more
With ears and nose and touch and in mind's eye
Than that slight spectrum that my eye's explore
Especially when I look for reasons why.

I s'pose both blind, and sighted, have to die
To see what's really there, beyond the sky.

Sonnet 101 (Eccentric)

In balance, moderation in all things.
Dead even. Steady, sure, between the lines
And prize the pleasure poise and coolness brings
All placid, calm and constant by designs.

Composed. Unruffled. Settled and serene.
Controlled, detached, contained and nonchalant
Confined and blessed, devoted to routine.
Full bridled, built by overcoming want.

These virtues, diamonds, that we value most
These merits, noted by the wise and great
Deny the wheel eccentric's wobbling boast
That genius is the will to innovate.

One hears, "Consistency, thou are a jewel"
But progress needs exceptions to that rule.

Sonnet 102 (War on Terror)

I guess what each of us would like to know
Is if somehow Dan Pearl is still alive.
We know he's captured by a dang'rous foe
And yet, a lot of hostages survive.

It's sad he even went to Pakistan
Investigating such a useless goon
As Richard Reid that friend of Taliban
Whose shoe bomb folly seems a mad cartoon.

What will we learn from all of this distress?
Dan Pearl is dead, or else, we hope, he's not
Yet others will be victims of this mess
And ere it's through, how many will be caught?

I have no faith that war will win this fight
My hope lies rather that we turn to right.

Sonnet 102 (Peace and War)

The price of anthrax keeps on going up
And bounty fit for kings is posted now
Against the hope of finding that mean pup
Who financed and romanced this terror show.

And we are all attuned to high alert
To distrust everyone and everything
As government officials reassert
That every weekend some new threat may bring.

I hope we do not take this proffered bait
And turn to soldiers, war and spies and such
To save us from the evil at our gate
Relying on these powers over-much.

A bit of this probably okay
But peace will only come another way.

Sonnet 103 (A King)

Most kings must wear a lonely heavy crown
Besieged by grasping sycophants and doubt
Not trusting those they see as they look down
And sensing that what lifts them, shuts them out.

The regal cannot be amidst the low
Or even walk among nobility
The monarch must maintain the royal show,
This is his grand responsibility.

These counterfeits of actual majesty
Trade any hope of happiness for power
Which makes an almost perfect guarantee
That such a foolish bargain will go sour.

Sometimes I think I'd like to be a king
Not thinking of the trouble that might bring.

Sonnet 105 (Force)

The peace a soldier brings is never sure
Police and guards and armies all are weak
No nation ever thus was made secure
Not Egypt, Rome or Jaredite, or Greek.

It wasn't Samson's muscles made him strong
Or David's skill with slings that sealed his fate
We falter when we turn from right to wrong
Not when our military strengths abate.

Still don't we need to build a force for good
To save us from the weapons of our foes
And give assurance that it's understood
We will not tolerate their wicked blows?

The greatest force for good is blessed with might
Not from an iron sword, but from the Light.

Sonnet 106 (Sometimes We Haply Wander)

Sometimes we haply wander where we will
Not keeping to a path or narrow way
But curious to learn each vale and hill
We rove and ramble free throughout the day.

Intoxicated by the wind and flowers
Intrigued by finding something ever new
We fail to take account of all these hours
In detour from the goals we still pursue.

Until the sunset catches us at last
Not only far from course and chosen trail
But also in that darkness overcast
That covers trav'lers caught behind the veil.

The signposts on the passageway to home
Obscured, through disregard, to those who roam.

Sonnet 107 (Salt Lake Olympics 2002)

We know the prophet claimed this place was right
And struck his cane to mark a temple spot
We see it guarded by the mountain height
And glory in the works great suffering brought.

We know an ancient saw it long before
And saw the nations flow unto its crown
And wrote great things we ought to not ignore
About the future of this Utah town.

Though flags from everywhere are now unfurled
To mark this place of ceremonial rites
This hosting of the finest in the world
Will be complete in just a few more nights.

While many places fade when this is done
We know this city's fame has just begun.

Sonnet 108 (Oh lost and fallen, castaway, and gone)

Oh lost and fallen, castaway, and gone
Oh beaten under foot of man and crushed
Oh shy and tender, fragile and withdrawn
Oh muted, voiceless, silenced. Muffled. Shushed.

I want to call you out and lift you up
To bless you and to bend and hold you near
I want to press your lips with heaven's cup
And wipe your brow of worry, pain, and fear.

I want to give you voice to make your plaint
To offer you my strength, my faith, my care,
To raise you from your sorrow to a saint
To take away, to add upon, to share.

I'll give and take, divide, and do my part
But it won't help unless you change your heart.

Sonnet 109 (Upon this day, Great Heaven's love descends)

Upon this day, Great Heaven's love descends
In dedicated, blessed, and hallowed vale
Beneath Olympic flame as loving friends
We name and bless this infant Thomson male.

And from the dust of Book of Mormon lands
A name declared as strong and brave and true
Defender of the lambs, he understands,
What virtue, courage, love and duty do.

Our Ammon, sweet and innocent and small
All new and fresh, a spark destined to burn
A promise, hope and mystery for all
Who wonder what will mark his earthly turn.

Well knowing, if he meets his given name
His light will be a true, eternal flame.

Sonnet 110 (There is no justice in this devil's land)

There is no justice in this devil's land
No recompense or healing for a wound
All void. An empty chair, an unseen hand
A barren home, no honour unimpugned.

No dignity, no fancy nor delight
No hope among unknown and lost and doomed
Despair that reigns unyielding day and night
Where dreams are damned and happiness consumed.

And yet in every cursed infernal space
One berth the devil cannot reach alone
Unless he's bidden by who owns the place
He cannot breach that part that's near the bone.

One day this world will see its great release
And from each heart will spread unbridled peace.

Sonnet 111 (The ice that clings to shadowed northern hills)

The ice that clings to shadowed northern hills
Is blown dark by dusty dirty air
And hides the fallen crevices it fills
Unyielding, mean and cold, devoid of care.

Like broken glass its former beauty's passed
It hunkers, hides and slinks away from sun
Unfeeling, doubting, bitter, frozen cast
It makes no move until the winter's done.

And even springtime changes it not much
Though finally dry valleys miles from
Will feel fresh icy water finger's touch
When longer day and higher noon have come.

So what is now congealed may some day boast
It didn't thaw until the need was most.

Sonnet 112 (The Frost man might extol the easy wind)

The Frost man might extol the easy wind
And marvel at the lovely downy flake
He might have pondered, might have slyly grinned
At winter's snowy devilish mistake.

And he might have been musing at the night
And how a choice for duty above sleep
Transcends the bitter urge to quit the fight
As he watched as the snowy woods grew deep.

But I've been thinking here as in my yard
The snow piles up and fills my drive with crud
And as the sidewalk's drifted high and hard
That time will turn this stuff to ice, then mud.

So as this storm descends upon my hovel
Instead of keeping promises, I shovel.

Sonnet 113 (The men are in the grocery store today.)

The men are in the grocery store today
Not many, but so many more than wives
They study lists with obvious dismay
What size of eggs? Where are the beans, the chives?

Outside the lot holds only four by fours
No cars can venture in this heavy snow
So dads are sent to do the shopping chores
While wild frigid winter blizzards blow.

These awkward hunter gatherers don't whine
They like this struggle with the drifted street
And battling with the elements is fine
Although they waver choosing Sunday's meat.

These days of difficult and extreme form
Define what may have once been more the norm.

Sonnet 114 (We sway above the perfect balance point)

We sway above the perfect balance point
We bend, we lean, we swing. We miss and hit
We're never quiet, always disappoint
We shift, we dodge, we duck. We grab we split.

We cross the fulcrum in a quickened state
And find our equilibrium is lost
And so it seems, our everlasting fate
To be as ocean waves by tempest tossed.

Still just the sense that balance can be had
And that a stable center place exists
Is quite enough to make a heart grow glad
And give it hope and comfort, as it twists.

So why not call it, "total vertigo"
The way it feels to live this life of woe?

Sonnet 115 (No murdered man has ever bothered me)

No murdered man has ever bothered me
No tortured ghost has haunted my abode
No specter chained has asked to be set free
No spell's decreed I should become a toad.

No cat that's black has changed my sort of luck
No charm has made me sleep a thousand years
I've never by a star or moon been struck
So these don't constitute my normal fears.

The things that bother me are more mundane,
Those creepy things like mice or snakes or flies
Or spilling stuff that's bound to leave a stain
Or sand between my toes or in my eyes.

But worse that bugs or dirt or ghouls or curses
Is trying to find rhymes for all these verses.

Sonnet 116 (I don't think anyone can say that they)

I don't think anyone can say that they
have never risen to the devil's bait,
have not become his apprehensive prey
or felt his hook against their wriggling weight.

Who has not wrestled manfully against
the nets of demon fishers hauling hard
or wasted precious strength while being fenced
by traps designed to catch us when off guard?

Yet in these murky waters there is light
that shines against the meanest wicked lures
exposing lines and barbs and snags of night
revealing what temptation's glare obscures.

What fun to be the quarry in this sea
And win the mortal struggle to be free.

Sonnet 117 (Anybody else having withdrawal pains after the Olympics?)

I watched the Putt Putt championship today
And lots of bowling for a healthy prize
And then to curling I was given sway
(The ladies kind, next week we see the guys).

Then as the day progressed the golf came on
Then basketball, both college and the pro
And in between the figure skaters shone
And skiers raced along the icy snow.

I even saw a spring league baseball game
And soccer from a country in the south
I found the polo match I watched too tame
But boxing and the football was smash-mouth.

Then hockey, NASCAR, fishing, then a break,
Recovering in twelve steps from Salt Lake.

Sonnet 118 (The eager hunter comes into our space)

The eager hunter comes into our space
Adjusts his eyes and focus to our light
He isn't looking for a resting place
He wants a restless victim in his sight.

We give no outward signal that we know
He's searching caref'lly for a certain prey
We hope by feigning that this isn't so
His hand upon us we may somehow stay.

Then fin'lly when he singles out his catch
He paralyzes it with just a glance
Then leads away the doomed and chosen wretch
While all the rest are sobered by this chance.

It ever will be thus, I do expec'
With that ward hunter that we call Exec.

Sonnet 119 (When Henry had his stroke at sixty eight)

When Henry had his stroke at sixty eight
And wasted for two years before he died
How could she guess the decades she would wait
Or count the countless lonely tears she's cried?

Surrounded only by the nursing staff
Bleak day resolves into a bitter night,
Like endless, grainless, fruitless, bits of chaff
Her emptiness filled up with empty rite.

And will she, living past allotted years,
While burying her children, one by one,
Develop an immunity to tears
Before her timeless time on earth is done?

I wonder if how long we take this test
Has any bearing on who bears it best?

Sonnet 120 (The world staggers on, all drunk with hate)

The world staggers on, all drunk with hate
A sloppy, cross, indifferent, peevish knave
Remembering the slights of ancient date
Forgetting what's heroic, good or brave.

A blaming, wanton, whining, spiteful sot
A careless, thoughtless, slack, dishonest sort
Destructive, brutal, cruel, overwrought
Impatient, restless, edgy, mean and short.

And both below and far above the fray
They suffer, one by one, who cannot leave
Or will not turn or even look away
But dream of better, sober, things. And grieve.

Unfair, iniquitous, unkind and blind
I guess we need this grind, to be refined.

Sonnet 121 (Sometimes we only see what isn't there)

Sometimes we only see what isn't there,
The shadow of a loss across sad eyes
The rudeness of a child lacking care
An empty heaven behind clear blue skies.

And always we are blind to what is real,
Bright eyes that hide a sorrow of the heart
Cold answers which don't answer, but conceal,
A trial which binds up what's come apart.

Our taste, our smelling, hearing, touch and sight
Betray us in the quest for higher things
They never get the universe quite right
And miss the best of what this moment brings.

Oh sure for baser stuff they serve us well
But wisdom's reach is far beyond their spell.

Sonnet 122 (We want our packages to be too neat)

We want our packages to be too neat
Exact, complete, secure and tied with string
We have an appetite for things too sweet
All sugary and safe and without sting.

We only want the rain to fall at night
We shy from things that rub or scratch or scrape
We want a tidy world that's crisp and tight
Amorphousness be gone, we call for shape.

Yet nature seems to make its masterpiece
With imprecise and casual use of time
It doesn't bend to form, it shows caprice,
It's loose with both its rhythm and its rhyme.

Our winter, this year, didn't come 'til spring
Could this mean we might dare a sim'lar thing?

Sonnet 123 (She asked my why my walk was such a mess)

She asked me why my walk was such a mess
And why the driveway ice was two feet high
She wondered why I seemed to not care less,
I answered with a slow contented sigh.

I'm trying to be virtuous and good
To conquer all my flaws and baser ways
To only be and do the things I should
And focus on what's worthy of high praise.

And since the sunny weather's coming soon
And all that ice and snow will melt okay,
I'm wise to rest my shovel until June.
I wish more people had my patient way.

Oh, all are sorely tempted once or twice
But patient men don't shovel snow or ice.

Sonnet 124 (I know these aged trees along the street)

I know these aged trees along the street
I ran beneath their branches years ago
And settled in their shade against the heat
On summer days when children's games grew slow.

I climbed among their younger supple arms
And hid behind bright leaves against the rain
I loved their sturdy trunks and leafy charms
Then left, and never thought of them again.

But now, a half a century gone by,
I walk again between my forest friends
And in the twinkling of my own mind's eye
I'm six years old, and childhood never ends.

Although the limbs are gnarled and bark gone grey
I cannot seem to see these trees that way.

Sonnet 125 (That cat that's sleeping down beside the park)

That cat that's sleeping down beside the park
Seems to be more than comfortably still
He doesn't move from morning until dark
Just what he does at night, I couldn't tell.

His bed is on a snow bank, and I'd guess
He would happier in a warmer place
But he does not complain or cause a fuss
So who am I to question choice of space?

I hope he knows that when the sun gets hot
His snowy home will disappear for good
And then he'll have to find another spot
To sleep away his hours in our 'hood.

If I was looking for a dog or cat
I think I'd choose a pet, at rest, like that.

Sonnet 126 (We often think that ignorance is bad)

We often think that ignorance is bad
And so we seek for knowledge all around
And as we learn we're satisfied and glad
With every bit of wisdom newly found.

But I have noticed that it isn't true
That only what we do not know can harm
The things we learn can oft times make us blue
And take from life the carefree things that charm.

This wisdom shows in men who never cook
Or women who stay strangers to the yard
Or misanthropes whose only friend's a book
Or klutzes who find chewing gum too hard.

But smartest of them all is that wise man
Who never learns a thing about a LAN.

Sonnet 127 (The regal feline pet may let you stay)

The regal feline pet may let you stay
As working guest or slave in her domain
But you must do your living in her way
Or she will make your house a house of pain.

A houseplant resting in a sunny nook
Demands small favours from its tending one
Or else it gets a brown and droopy look
And lets its crispy leaves become undone.

A plastic fern resplendent in a pot
Will grace a humble house with splash of green
And sit contently in any spot
And never beg for water or cuisine.

Between the cat, the houseplant, and the fake
I'm never troubled choosing which to take.

Sonnet 128 (To follow in the dust of greater men)

To follow in the dust of greater men
And choke upon the product of their schemes
And be obedient and faithful when
Your vision is reduced to hopes and dreams.

To think no ill of what you cannot know
Yet still defines your fate and steals your force
And watch and feel as difficulties grow
That test your dedication to the course.

To be the first to want and last to get
To pray and pray and pray and pray some more
Then mix your boiling blood with tears and sweat
And still see others going on before.

This makes you chosen master of the last
And heir to final glory unsurpassed.

Sonnet 129 (The most of what we say is meant to cure)

The most of what we say is meant to cure
The least of what we said sometime before
I'm sure if we could speak Adamic pure
And had our hearts unsullied to the core

We wouldn't have to try to overcome
The stupid thoughtless things we say so much
Or feel so often desperate and dumb
Because our hearts and tongues are out of touch.

And then there's all the times we're silent when
We ought to give a word of honest cheer
Or send a warning out to save a friend
Who's lost or paralyzed by sin or fear.

A skill that everyone of us should seek
Is how and what and where and when to speak.

Sonnet 130 (The heart can sometimes feel what eyes can't see)

The heart can sometimes feel what eyes can't see
And driving by myself across the land
I felt just what had been and what might be
Much more than seeing helped me understand.

Confusion, haste, and business all undone
At Independence, marked my moment there,
Though at Far West the beauty of the sun
Broke through the sorrow of Missouri's air.

The chill at Council Bluff was not as cold
But twice as sharp as made Wyoming brave
And Nauvoo's brilliant temple, fresh and bold
A promise like hope Ondi-Ahman gave.

Still, for me, Carthage, has that special feel
So bittersweet. So intimate. So real.

Sonnet 131 (Parable of the gift basket)

The little basket, full of soaps and stuff
To clean and freshen up a body's scent
Was given with a lesson, kind not tough,
And meant to help an offender repent.

Her odor chased away the chance for friends
And so a teacher, helping, loving, thought
That such a gift might start more happy trends
And felt quite hopeful as the deed was wrought.

But when the class was over came the child
And gave the basket back with willing hands
"These things I'll never use or need." she smiled,
And shattered all the teacher's well made plans.

I wonder when like gifts are given to me
If I return them just as handily?

Sonnet 132 (The Hubble is a tiny crack of light)

The Hubble is a tiny crack of light
That leads the mind to things it cannot count
Infinity and worlds beyond our sight
And possibilities without account.

This outward reach that reasoning transcends
By challenging our grasp of time and place
Suggests we understand that nothing ends
There is no stop or border to our space.

Still, what is even harder for my mind
Is looking to the infinitely small
To know that sub atomically confined
No universe is smallest of them all.

There is no end to endless, great or low
Or to the things we hope to someday know.

Sonnet 133 (Some children live for only just a while)

Some children live for only just a while
Mere visitors not really part of us
Perhaps they've proved themselves without this trial
Not needing but a touch of all this fuss.

It wounds us when they get their final call
We grieve and fret and feel the hand of pain
Invested as we are in loving all
It hurts, but it's our duty to remain.

We know they meet with glory where they go
They lose no blessings from their shortened stay
And leave their touch of heaven's love below
To spark resolve to live a better way.

So one day when our earthly stay is done
Brief guests and us can once again be one.

Sonnet 134 (He dares but say the things that matter most)

He dares but say the things that matter most
That slice one open like a thousand wounds
And build up as a force too strong to host
And which all sensibility impugns.

No time to speak of lesser needless things
To prattle, blather, natter or to chat
Less even is he wont to speak of kings
Or war, or politics or things like that.

His voice, too close, too cold, for gentle ears
No sweetness telegraphs an easy lie
Nor flattering to cover empty fears
His is a piercing, mean, defiant cry.

Still better to keep listening and learn
Than ever from guilt's importuning turn.

Sonnet 135 (My sorrow is a village in my heart)

My sorrow is a village in my heart
With streets unpaved and fallen garden walls
Where nothing's whole and everything's apart,
With murky plots, where bitter drizzle falls.

The air is cold with winter's deadly chill
And sunlight's healing beam is never found
Across the village highway to the hill
That highway which no detour goes around.

The city on the hill, my summer place,
Full gladness makes its happy home within,
Cannot be gained unless I win the race
By passing through those villages of sin.

My joy is a city in my breast
Eternal, warm, and where I hope to rest.

Sonnet 136 (A birdie's nest is built with twigs and mud)

A birdie's nest is built with twigs and mud
A fox may lightly renovate a hole
And fish live unencumbered in the flood
While bridge embankments satisfy the troll.

To cover up his underwater pad
A beaver dams a stream to make a pond
And turtles in their very homes are clad
And bats and rats, of caves, seem to be fond.

While more or less attention must be paid
To build a shelter in a tree or ditch
The greatest architectural plans are laid
To satisfy that human housing itch.

Oh, even busy beavers must admire
The way we build much more than we require.

Sonnet 137 (A sonnet every second day will make)

A sonnet every second day will make
Three sonnets plus a half for every week
And figuring that pace at month end break
That makes it 15 sonnets, so to speak.

Yet every month is not precisely split
As some months add one day while just one lacks
The days to make those 15 sonnets fit
So write the 15 sonnets, then relax.

Thus 15 sonnets every month will sum
One hundred eighty by the end of year
And though the most may bore you and be dumb
Perhaps a couple may amuse and cheer.

It's funny how by doing bit by bit
We get a lot more done than if we quit.

Sonnet 138 (Let every song of life be understood)

Let every song of life be understood
Like harmony and melody combined
Let music and pure logic be one good
And music's mathematic thrill the mind.

Let nuance and straightforwardness be one
And subtlety be just the same as plain
And every poem be just a bit of fun
Let nothing ever tax or try the brain.

Forget the many shades of light and sound
That test degrees of meaning against form
Don't study what lies hidden 'neath the ground
By digging at the lies we call "the norm".

Let's make each song, though clever, clear and pure
Far better to be shallow, than obscure.

Sonnet 139 For Sam Payne

The shadow on the wall in rhythm with
Excited dancing strings and melodies
That wash across the night time like a myth
Sweet tunes that challenge, beckon, kiss and tease.

Above, a child sleeps in harmony
Not knowing life without his home of song
A captive never wanting to break free
From music's early web, so fine and strong.

The siren violin in mother's hand
The guitar wrapped in father's loving arms
Their passion, now his spark, is thusly fanned
Until it flames and welds him to its charms.

Beware of making shadow music waves
Unless you want your children to be slaves.

Sonnet 140 (The patient early winter river flows)

The patient early winter river flows
All dark and cold and heavy as a stone
And out of roiling, steaming water grows
The ice that sets this fluid into bone.

Then springtimes splashing reckless rolling flood
A rough and carving carrier of all
This teeming flotsam bed of liquid mud
Destined to build up deltas in its stall.

Then summer sun bursts down from endless sky
And waters selflessly relax their hold
To run more clear and clean throughout July.
Ignoring how the fall should bring new cold.

Each year the river's life is thus made whole
Yet some still doubt it has a heart and soul.

Sonnet 141 (She wears her bright red jacket every day)

She wears her bright red jacket every day
A scarlet sign, at once, of life and death
To bleed, to live, to die, to plead, to pray
The very fountain out of which flows breath.

She sees, though flesh and bone, through heavy lead
And penetrates the pretense of this night
Much stronger than mere muscle or great dread
The seed of coming nations clothed in might.

There are so many millions blessed the same
That what she is and does seems common fare
But sisterhood should not dilute her name
This precious brilliant ruby solitaire.

We dare not worship any but divine
But still the blood red woman is a shrine.

Sonnet 142 (I've gone to kneel among the stately pines)

I've gone to kneel among the stately pines
Where mountain snows lie deep and cool and white
And where, it seems, the moon light always shines
To make an endless day of every night.

I've gone to kneel where no one else has knelt
When no one but the wind moved round about
And where, it seems, the something that I felt
Has turned great heaven's whisper to a shout.

Thus far from light of human daily life
The stars shine brighter, stronger, closer too
And soon forgotten is the petty strife
Which clouds my heart's desire for what's true.

I've gone to kneel among the stately pines
And where, it seems, the moon light always shines.

Sonnet 143 (I watch and listen without love or care)

I watch and listen without love or care
to arguments that matter just to them
unwilling to defend, assert, or share
and feeling, by my silence, to condemn.

I judge their wrangling as too small and trite
to occupy my interest or concern,
yet never let them quite get out of sight
and even, sometimes, itch to take a turn.

This habit makes firm foes of once fast friends
its shadow always longer than its light
and tragic is how frequent such talk ends
with both sides wronged and neither being right.

To help me overcome temptation's rule
please argue out of earshot from this fool.

Sonnet 144 (We sometimes have to close our eyes to see)

We sometimes have to close our eyes to see
To shut out blinding everyday displays,
To view what was or what may someday be
We have to filter out existing rays.

The now is such a short and narrow way
To stay there constantly restricts our sight
While infinite and splendid the array
That past and future visions can make bright.

Still, daydreaming can bear a heavy cost
If we don't learn what instant moments teach
And much of what is wonderful is lost
To those for whom the present's out of reach.

I search for balance in the time I spend
Between what's here and now, and what's pretend.

Sonnet 145 (I have to say for quite a while I tried)[iii]

I have to say for quite a while I tried
To figure out these threats to world peace
To sort out animosity and pride
And judge suggestions made to help war cease.

Afghanistan, al Qaeda, Taliban
Israelis, PLO and Arafat
Iran, Iraq and surly Pakistan
With buses and Ramallah blown flat.

I had to look to CNN and such
To tell me every day what happened next
And I was happy to be kept in touch
And tried to keep these issues in context.

But now! The only news they'll give or take
Is stuff about that actor Robert Blake!

Sonnet 146 (We take a singing bird into our space)

We take a singing bird into our space
And keep her safe and watered, fed and warm
Although she's caged she knows she owns this place
And lives her life secure in song and charm.

Her lustrous lemon yellow feathered coat
Is lightning in our home of rose and cream
And what comes trilling from her tiny throat
Is to sopranos like a brilliant dream.

We cover her against the morning light
To save us from announcements of the dawn
And hope she isn't angered by the slight
When we pull back her blanket with a yawn.

Captivity, I guess, was not her choice
But still there's cheerful beauty in her voice.

Sonnet 147 (Old Gameliel, he had it figured out)[iv]

Old Gameliel, he had it figured out -
"This work, if it be just of men will come
To absolutely naught. But this I'll shout,
If it's of God, to fight it would be dumb!"

And so the wheels of time have turned and now
We see what Gameliel was saying then
Expressed in this prophetic, fateful vow
"What man tears down our God will build again."

The place is small and humble, almost quaint,
She bears a certain sadness in her soul
This village, once a city for the Saint,
Prepares herself to once again be whole.

And so THIS twenty seventh day of June
Will finally mark a joyful afternoon.

Sonnet 148 (I have a deal for someone. Something cheap!)

I have a deal for someone. Something cheap!
And though it's really precious as can be
You will not have to scrounge or dig too deep
Cuz what I'm dealing here is going free.

I won't be asking anything at all
And even that is FOB your place
Delivery will be "special" not "you call"
And you can even have a few days grace.

It's kinda heavy, sorry about that
And it may crowd you just a bit and close
But at the price I hope you'll find it phat
And take it from me even if it's gross.

This thing you get's superfluous, you see
What's gotta go is fifty pounds of me.

Sonnet 149 (I try to keep from scratching at my itch)

I try to keep from scratching at my itch
By firmly telling Scratch to "get behind"
And acting like I haven't heard his pitch
Ignoring when he strives to win my mind.

I sometimes even use a salve of sorts
To minimize the yearnings of my nights
Distracting me from all his mean resorts
I cover up and thus avoid the fights.

I hope I'm like a tree that needs the wind
To make its early roots and trunk grow strong
So later on it's able to rescind
The gales that seek to blow from right to wrong.

And so I keep adjusting my attack
To get that prickly fellow off my back.

Sonnet 150 (Each Wednesday is a triumph of its own)

Each Wednesday is a triumph of its own
A tribute to the victory of time
A fulcrum where the middle point is shown
Where each descent begins anew to climb.

A crack between what was and what will be
The dawn and dusk between the dark and night
And so it's not surprising, not to me,
We live our lives in search of Wednesday night.

Of course we know of some who find it dull
This day of mediocrity sublime
They say they want their cup of life more full
They thrive on the extremities of time.

I raise a cheer for what each Wednesday brings
This prince of moderation in all things.

Sonnet 152 (Come. Take a turn with me across the floor)

Come. Take a turn with me across the floor
we'll swing and sway, and slide and lift, and glide.
Come. Dance and dance and dance. And dance some more
Come, let the music be our only guide.

Surrender to the rhythm and the song
of sweating, heaving bodies in this trance
and prove the possibilities all wrong
by steady, constant, "larger than life" dance.

The time to rest and settle will come soon
enough. Our rhythm will go bad and be
too rough. The sun will chase away the moon
s'great bluff, and set all foolish dancer's free.

Come. Take a turn with me across the floor.
Come dance. And dance and dance. And dance some more.

Sonnet 151 (The dreams that haunt the driven, day and night)

The dreams that haunt the driven, day and night,
The wanton boasts of future conquests fought
That better measure fate than honest fight
And spoil the glory of triumphs unsought.

Who sells these phantom wishes as a good,
Who tempts the common man to reach too far
To try to capture flags he never could
Or waste his earthy vision on a star?

But no one's lifted without looking up
We always go towards our line of sight
And if he never earns the victor's cup
At least the dreamer's face is to the light.

On altars of illusion, sacrificed,
Are those thus foolishly enticed.

Sonnet 153 (I wonder if they turned me inside out)

I wonder if they turned me inside out
Or if they carefully peeled away my skin
Would there be room to speculate or doubt
About what secrets might be found within?

I like to think I'm something more than dust
That's organized to make a living clay
And that this body's actually just a crust
For something unaffected by decay.

I 'spect I'm quite like every other stiff
All full of blood and bones and flesh and fat
But searching there, no one could get a whiff
Of what I really am, or things like that.

Besides, for now, an autopsy would be
A bit of inconvenience for me.

Sonnet 154 (Some things that happened long ago I keep)

Some things that happened long ago I keep
In memory as obvious as day
To call upon in comfort, stress, or sleep
To hedge me up and decorate my way.

While other things I haply have forgot,
Just what they are, I really could not say,
But sadly if they're lessons cruelly taught,
I risk again becoming easy prey.

They say it's best to keep a written leaf
Of all our doings, good, or bad, or fey
And thus combat remembrance's thief
Who gathers us so gently in his sway.

And so since I approach that certain age
I have to wonder, who will read my page?

Sonnet 155 (The fires burn in Bethlehem today)

The fires burn in Bethlehem today
Millennia of hate and hot distrust
Are signaled by a conflagrant display
As prejudice and passion now combust.

The outrage and the fury unrestrained
As terror, dread and hopelessness are wrought
And mothers' eyes are drawn tight and pained
As vengeance as a virtue now is taught.

It's more than irony that death and war
Are centered now upon the manger site
For nothing can be hoped from battle's roar
Yet every hope began here, on that night.

And I'm quite sure the church that's on this spot
Will go, now... or, when things get really hot

Sonnet 156 A Sonnet for My Daughter

Some ask the world for fame or praise or gold
Some worry and concern their every friend
Some act with reckless passion, overbold,
Demanding. Needing. Asking without end.

While others, rare and charming by contrast
Are born to give, to help, to raise, to bind
To hold, to care, to lift from first to last
To be all tenderheartedness.. and kind.

A blessing to this father, above all,
To have a daughter thusly good and strong
Who stands in beauty singularly tall
And sings in tune with heaven's lovely song.

Her wisdom, humor, modesty and love
Remind, on earth, of virtues found above.

Sonnet 157 (Though iron bars may guard a prison cell)

Though iron bars may guard a prison cell
And keep a prisoner from reaching out
They hardly could be doing their job well
While letting in abundant fear and doubt.

Deprived of simple freedoms behind bars
The captive, still, is never safe from hate
And unattended woundings bring such scars
They curse imprisoned souls and violate.

But who, enslaved or not, is ever free
From injury and pain and awful smear
And who, confined or not, could hope to be
Protected from the slights of doubt and fear?

And in the end the only way to cope
Is by embracing, fully, faith and hope.

Sonnet 158 (I tell the tale of winter come to stay)

I tell the tale of winter come to stay
Of cold, cold wind and frost and snow and ice
Of clouds that block out any sunny ray
Of feeling trapped in wintry weather's vise.

I tell the tale of blizzards as the norm
When gentle, warm and sweet cannot describe
And talk of temperance is out of form
And temperate people threaten to imbibe.

I tell the story of an April/May
That made a normal January blush
And set a standard for a winter day
That beat it like a gambler's royal flush.

But still, of course, you will not hear me whine
Since we all know this moisture is divine.

Sonnet 159 (I hope one day to rise and write the song)

I hope one day to rise and write the song
Of every promise May and June can make
The lyric tender, passionate, yet strong
The melody that deepest thoughts awake.

Another ode to spring is not enough
Some greater, better music should prevail
Than all that charming, sweet and simple stuff
That bound like tiny boats with too much sail.

But though I have the feeling for this task
And hold the need and scope within my heart
And yearn to tear away the season's mask
I know I lack the talent for this art.

Still, May and June deserve a better rant
Than sugar coated odes can ever grant.

Sonnet 160 (I've been awake now for about a day)

I've been awake now for about a day
I've seen the sun come up, then start to leave
I've done a bit of work, and had some play
And now I've got to knit back up my sleeve.

And so I start what takes about three hours
A ritual that seems to grow each year
A rain of reading, flossing and of showers
Of pills and prayers and exercise severe.

A time to see the doors are all secure
To lotion up what's dry and clip my nails
To change into pajamas and make sure
I've covered all my pre-sleeping details.

Sometimes I think I spend less time asleep
Than all of this. Plus counting those darn sheep.

Sonnet 161 (The lie is everywhere professed as true)

The lie is everywhere professed as true
That prizes of the earth will make us glad
And so we hardly know what else to do
But strive to get as much as can be had.

And earth yields up her cache of treasured wares
To any who through luck or skill or might
Are able to declare the goods as theirs
And prove that declaration with a fight.

Tis heaven holds the keys to earthly joy
It rains down blessings in a constant way
We only need to learn the wise employ
Of instruments for catching heaven's ray.

The tools to bring us bliss are not the same
As those we use to grub for gold or fame.

Sonnet 162 (The cool glance may hide the heated heart)

The cool glance may hide the heated heart
The casual wink disguise the constant thought
The nod may bind what cannot come apart
The smile veil the soul that's overwrought.

We think we have the sense of what goes on
Behind the masks that men and women wear
And thus we often reach an end foregone
With judgments less of wisdom than of dare.

Such fleeting looks and winks and nods and smiles
Are given for a reason, I suppose,
But if they pass on less of truth than wiles
It only means you cannot trust what shows.

I don't suppose a gesture meant to hide
The truth, is quite the same is if one lied.

Sonnet 163 (The humble voice is quick to fade away)

The humble voice is quick to fade away
At once, its feeble sound is come then gone
It's not the sort of thing that's meant to stay
All talk is just an instant, then withdrawn.

And what we say should always stand the gauge
Of adding more to life than silence would
Of being (more than quiet), kind and sage
Of being (more than nothing) understood.

But though the tongue be cruel or untamed
To silence it would cost a heavy price
As many guilty would remain unnamed
If capable of keeping this advice.

I'll ponder here a bit before I speak
For me, a rather new, untried technique.

Sonnet 164 (I like to keep my options open wide)

I like to keep my options open wide
To never close off paths I might pursue
It isn't that I shift from side to side
Or that I can't decide what's right and true.

It's more a case of wanting everything
Of holding on to all the stuff I can
And so I'm awfully slow to give a fling
To what I hope might someday fit my plan.

It's better far to be decisive and
To toss off baggage not in present need
To never worry about what's unplanned
Or give unlikely choices any heed.

Still all this clutter kind of grows on me
And so I think I'll keep my options free.

Sonnet 165 (I pull my paddle through the wet with ease)

I pull my paddle through the wet with ease
And glide along. The seashore as my guide,
I make adjustments for the freshening breeze
And keep the open water to my side.

I could be quicker to my journey's end
If I would set a course more in the deep
Ignore each inefficient wandering bend
And make the most of every paddle sweep.

But things I see along the water's edge
Look better to me than the troubling sea
And beckon like the siren's wanton pledge
To satisfy and set this paddler free.

And even, sometimes, I am tempted to
Slide into shore and quit this frail canoe.

Sonnet 166 (Oh fickle wishes. How to tame your call!)

Oh fickle wishes. How to tame your call!
And break the tie of passion's perverse cord
To wrestle wanting's agitated squall
And earn the fruits of patience for reward.

I guess that no one really ever knows
If what he wants today might soon become
As troubling anxious anguish often shows
The very thing he next desires undone.

But honest hearts must follow their desires
And doubting that our vital wants will last
Is quenching to the soul's most basic fires
And forces us to live in glories past.

It's best to bridle, not to stifle, hope
And keep our balance on this two way slope.

Sonnet 167 (A flash of lightening in the late May sky)

A flash of lightening in the late May sky
And thunder shakes the air in chorus bold
It should be raining, wild and hard and high,
But somehow, it's all snow and wind and cold.

The seasons upset, inside out, and lost
Apocalyptic, tragic, new and wrong
A mixed up day that's cast in crazy frost
Instead of sun and spring time's tender song.

These days will come from time to time by chance
When work and school and daily routine stops
When all the rhythm of our treadmill dance
Is pushed towards a dangerous brink. Then drops.

Oh what the heck, just take it as a gift
The journey back to normal will be swift.

Sonnet 168 (He carried extra laces for his boots)

He carried extra laces for his boots
And kept a band-aid in his billfold too
He always bought those trusty two pants suits
And never chanced to stand in his canoe.

He always measured twice before he cut
And lived to mend with stitches done in time
The doors that kept his cows were ever shut
And everything he said was said in rhyme.

His teeth were flossed and Water Pic'd each day
His mitten string was kept in perfect trim
He never tried to swim with his toupee
Nor would he ever go out on a limb.

And since his prudence seemed to know no ends
It's hardly strange to find he had no friends.

Sonnet 169 (Why lift a rock for what is hidden there?)

Why lift a rock for what is hidden there?
The dark and dank are satisfied beneath
They never struggle, it would seem, for air
Or wash a grimy face or brush their teeth.

High pressure cleansing isn?t what they want
Nor even will they hail the light of day
It's somber, cool and quiet in their haunt
And they are there because that suits their way.

I guess we like to kick and turn those stones
And scatter feckless creatures in their fright
In hopes ambition sleeping in their bones
Will wake upon exposure to the light.

And even as we kick at wormy beds
Are there not rocks above our soiled heads?

Sonnet 170 (The wind won't listen to me when I whine)

The wind won't listen to me when I whine
It seems to notice nothing of my plight
It makes its song oblivious to mine
Ignoring my complaining day and night.

The rain disdains my tears as trifling drops
It makes its floods or hides from desert sands
According to its will it starts or stops
Unmindful of my wants or my commands.

The sun may be unbending, but it's fair
It comes and goes on schedule like a clock
Each day it does its pleasant work with flare
A faithful shepherd to a distant flock.

The doubtful wind and rain may do their part
But only sunshine owns the honest heart.

Sonnet 171 (The world I understand is quite petite)

The world I understand is quite petite
It occupies a corner of my mind
Nor would I ever say that it was neat,
It's mostly full of stuff I cannot find.

The world which I cannot comprehend
Surrounds me like eternal atmospheres
No boundaries to where it might extend
Encompass all my deficits and fears.

Yet vastness of the things misunderstood
Defines importance of what may be known
And makes extremely precious as a good
Those tiny bits of wisdom, rarely shown.

The trouble is, with all I have to learn,
I'm quickly running out of time to burn.

Sonnet 172 (I think umbrellas on the stage are nice)

I think umbrellas on the stage are nice
The way they spin and hypnotize the crowd
A clever choreographer's device
A mask, a whirling curtain, and a shroud.

I like umbrellas folded as a cane
Proud walking sticks, so elegant, so chic,
They make a clumsy feller feel urbane
And ordinary strollers look unique.

Umbrellas in the wind don't count for much
They flip, they rip, they tip, then slip your grip
Unkeeled, unruddered, all untamed and such
Like sails without a proper mast or ship.

Umbrellas come in every shade and size
And in a quiet rain they're quite a prize.

Sonnet 173 (Picasso made his fortune out of form)

Picasso made his fortune out of form
His palate and perspective seemed so new
He didn't ever pander to the norm
And even changed himself to rose from blue.

His art like poetry intent with rhymes
And sunburned soldiers ever filled with hurt
Defied the human need for shade, at times,
When men live out their lives without a shirt.

He loved to decorate a simple pot
Or draw an acrobat above the crowd
Or paint downtrodden women, so distraught
Their pain and terror seems to shout out loud.

Still I must be a philistine and rube
Because I've never understood the cube.

Sonnet 174 (It helps to have a goal in mind I think)

It helps to have a goal in mind I think
To want for something reachable, but dear,
There has to be the concept of the brink
That sense of liability and fear.

A risk/reward analysis is nice
But must include a deadline for the climb
And every calculation of the price
Should take into account the cost in time.

Still of the sort who never get things done
We find a lot with planners close at hand
Although they're almost always on the run
It seems as if their feet are in quicksand.

It seems there's something deeper to the test
Than using all the tools of Franklin Quest.

Sonnet 175 (I've lost my faith before, then got it back)

I've lost my faith before, then got it back
I've wandered, wasted, stumbled, gone astray,
And little even did I want that track
But somehow found again the better way.

I've staggered to the edge, then turned around
I've feared the height then backed off from the fall
I've gone off course but still come back to ground
And been redeemed before I lost it all.

And though I glory in these saving times
And grateful am for being snatched from death
My confidence is tested by my crimes
And doubt and worry rage in every breath

Anxiety is part of safety too
Its power has a hand in staying true.

Sonnet 176 (A sonnet every day in June is fine)

A sonnet every day in June is fine
To celebrate the best a year can be
Anticipating at a natural shrine
The glory which provokes the bended knee.

This song of summer's advent and its stay
With melodies of migrants from afar
This promise of a better, kinder day
The calendar's resplendent polar star.

A month that's strangely out of touch with death
Too verdant, lush and new to be believed
Impossible as birth and baby's breath
It won't be lost or wrong or small or grieved.

June's cheerful summer solstice blooms anew
And all the world is right and fresh and true.

Sonnet 177 (It's quite a lot of fun to speculate)

It's quite a lot of fun to speculate
To guess about some changes on the way
And try to pick a likely candidate
To occupy an office for a day.

We always like to try to sort among
What favorite might get the final nod
Or wonder if it might be one... unsung,
A darkhorse or a longshot... someone odd.

Then whether we are wrong, or if we're right,
In guessing who receives the blessed call
We shake his trembling hand and hug him tight
Then walk away and leave him in the hall.

Cause once the man is called the game is done
And that's the end of speculating fun.

Sonnet 178 (We had almost a thousand screamings kids)

We had almost a thousand screaming kids
To witness as the rockets blasted off
And chase the remnants of these astral bids
And cheer success and at the fizzles scoff.

I guess we launched three dozen, maybe more
And then a rocket wrecked right on the pad
It shook and twisted wickedly before
It shot across the playground hot and mad.

It came about a yard or two from me
Before it stopped its frenzied drunken rush
And for an instant no one seemed to see
And we were like dumb chickens.... all a hush.

Then suddenly one student... howling... pained!
The random rocket's victim ascertained.

Sonnet 179 (The tall grass tangles in my tired feet)

The tall grass tangles in my tired feet
And trips me roughly to the cruel ground
Without the narrow smoothness of the street
No certain path to safety can be found.

Beneath this nervous crest of windblown grass
I press my anxious face against the earth
And wonder when and how this day will pass
And will it end in death or with rebirth.

I roll upon my back and hunt the sun
But all I see is blue, eternal blue
I'll have to lift my head, then try to run
And hope the light that finds me turns out true.

I draw another breath in hidden pain
Then rise up suddenly and run again.

Sonnet 180 (I'm snuggled in a cotton batting bath)

I'm snuggled in a cotton batting bath
My senses stuffed with wool and fire in one
A victim of some tiny microbe's wrath
My goose is more than cooked, it's overdone.

I'm tippy, wonky, staggering and faint
I'm cloudy, foggy, slow and overcast
I hesitate to make this a complaint
But now my eyes aren't focusing, they're glassed!

I could go home and take a proper pill
To put an end to notice of my pain
But if I did then how could I fulfill
My duty to extend this flu-like chain?

Tis better to be giving than to get
And so I'll put some others in my debt.

Sonnet 181 (He carries angel wings upon his back)

He carries angel wings upon his back
And walks the valley floor without a care
The road is smooth, a broad and easy track
His destination clear, yet far, up there.

The trail grows narrow as he comes to hills
And winding now, between the rocks and trees
He has to call on navigating skills
And fix upon the stars from bended knees.

At last he gains the splendid target peak
His broken heart so happy that it sings.
His breath, so forced, he's lost the gift to speak
He stands a moment. Then he spreads his wings

One step between the valley and the light
Will launch his final solitary flight.

Sonnet 182 Considering Proverbs 14:29[v]

Some come to boil rapidly enough
To wholly miss the joy of growing warm
Their flashing point is more than just a bluff
They miss completely expectation's charm.

Without a clutch to temper anger's drive
The race to rage is rapid beyond sense
And ties that keep society alive
Are ripped asunder by the least offense.

But when the process is controlled and slow
The trigger seldom trips that ends debate
And understanding, with a chance to grow,
Will yield a blessing wonderful and great.

A hasty spirit marks the common fool
While wisdom follows him who keeps his cool.

Sonnet 183 Considering Proverbs 17:28[vi]

The judgment of a man depends on this,
That there be ought to judge the man upon,
And therefore silent subjects have this bliss
That peace is ever more the pro than con.

And so the quiet man is counted wise
His stillness a priori must be good
No one can suffer character demise
Unless he deigns to say more than he should.

But if we all would take this good advice
And shut our lips against the wish to speak
The silence, for a while, might seem nice
But, in the end, a tiresome technique.

So I say, spit it out, let's hear your heart.
Who knows, it just may prove you smart.

Sonnet 184 (I wonder. Should I make this daring plan?)

I wonder. Should I make this daring plan?
Make it my strong and passionate desire
Set back some things I may have just began
And push this scheme into my hottest fire.

I have the notion, only, just right now
It isn't anything I have to do
I haven't put my hand yet to the plough
I could just put this off and still be true.

And why not just decide to make a try
Not bind myself to pledges and to time
Why am I thinking like I have to buy
When borrowing or renting is no crime?

But dreams can really only get a start
When schemes turn into cov'nants of the heart.

Sonnet 185 (The wind leans heav'ly on my garden wall)

The wind leans heav'ly on my garden wall
Intruding in to study what is mine
And sometimes sections of my wall will fall
Obscuring what I hoped would mark a line.

My neighbor has no fence or even hedge
He seems to urge invasions of his space
And since there' nothing which defends his edge
The wind will wander wildly through his place.

Good fences make good neighbors, so it's said,
And mending garden walls is healing toil
And golden is the fine and perfect thread
That separates without dividing soil.

The wind and rain and sun will always find
Some way to breach the garden of the mind.

Sonnet 186 (The plots of land we subdivide for us)

The plots of land we subdivide for us
Imaginary though they be in fact
Seem able to stir up a lot of fuss
And test the weakness of the social pact.

Most wars are fought to gain or keep our lands
And even next door neighbors sometimes fight
To qualify the bargains for these sands
That shift between the hourglass of might.

Sometimes we try to trade some land for peace
To make a foe a friend by giving ground
Or help an ally with a lend or lease
In hopes an easy answer can be found.

But souls that hunger for that greater plot
Are seldom satisfied until we're naught.

Sonnet 187 (So now, we, everyone, has access to)

So now, we, everyone, has access to
The secrets of the universe revealed
We have the means to find the good and true
To have our futures sanctified and sealed.

We, all, are blessed in kind by heaven's gift
And shouldn't know the weight of sin or fear
There's really no requirement to sift
The path to follow's marvelously clear.

But still, we, many, dither as we go
Or fight or sleep, or wander or make fun
Our curiosity for what's below
Is greater than attraction to the sun.

We, everyone, will waste and wear away
And choose, by doing, how the end will play.

Sonnet 188 (The structure of the brain is known to man)

The structure of the brain is known to man
The lobes and hemispheres are mapped for use
We even probe and test and eas'ly scan
To find the signs of sickness and abuse.

And we can measure power of the mind
Intelligence by quotient and degree
And yet it's very difficult to find
The who or what, that holds all wisdom's key.

It won't be found with MRI's and such
Or even among Mensa's lofty kind,
No part of medicine can help us much
To raise the thinking level of mankind.

There is a place where wisdom gets its start
But don't look in the head. It's in the heart.

Sonnet 189 (It started, piled near my basement door)

It started, piled near my basement door
It always seemed to get into the way
I've moved it many times before
And now I've moved it once again today.

The pine, the scout troop sold to fund a camp
The birch, a victim of my friend's caprice,
The spruce, now black and sodden from the damp,
I know that woodpile, almost piece by piece.

This time I chose the furthest corner spot
Against my backyard fence, to stack the wood
And now it's settled there, I hope, to rot,
And that my woodpile moving's done for good.

It's hard sometimes to find the perfect place
To keep those things acquired "just in case".

Sonnet 191 (I'll take my day in yellow in anytime)

I'll take my day in yellow anytime
It's brighter than the brown or even blue
It looks much better than the red or lime
And seems, than orange, to be much more true.

It's sunny, warm and lively to the touch
It penetrates and radiates and shines
I like its cheerful nature very much
It makes me think of symbols, types and signs.

Of course this preference is just my own
It's not a thing to proselytize about
And yet, what other color can be shone
To scatter every shadow of a doubt?

I revel in each smiling yellow day
Exhilarated by each golden ray.

Sonnet 190 (Who has not roughly, finally, swept away)

Who has not roughly, finally, swept away
The scattered remnants of his better work?
The cast off leavings kept for but a day
The margin notes of every perfect clerk.

The hopeful fragments of unfinished poems
The dust of marble monuments to art.
Blue penciled out of any scholar's tomes
Ideas once held sacred in his heart.

Will heaven bless again if by design
We fail to keep a notion from above
And lose some earth sent gift from the divine
Because we failed to guard it with our love?

Be honest. Do you keep that mess around
Because within it nuggets may be found?

Sonnet 192 (The Sunday morning stillness of the past)

The Sunday morning stillness of the past
When heavy tranquil summer air was king
Is broken by the throbbing and the blast
Of leaf blowers and trimmers whipping string.

The time when bells would peel their solo songs
To pilgrims gathering for hymns and prayer
Has given way to choruses from lawns
As mowers fill the summer Sabbath air.

And those who once were restless in their beds
As dawn gave way to morning, then to noon
Who felt the call to bow their sinful heads
Will likely be up, mowing, sometime soon.

Then fin'lly when the yard work all is done
It's time to find a way to have some fun.

Sonnet 193 (The man is glib, articulate and smooth) [vii]

The man is glib, articulate and smooth
He seems to be intelligent and kind
Celebrities and senators he'll sooth
And 15 minute fame seekers he'll find.

He never challenges or makes ashamed
He doesn't ever pounce upon a lie
He doesn't look for someone to be blamed
He wants to be a friend, he'll never pry.

And so the world opens to his face
And we all watch, relaxed and half asleep,
Amazed at how he manages his pace
And skips about from trivia to deep.

I think his secret is he listens well
This King who casts a nightly talk show spell.

Sonnet 194 (Did Spencer K and Mother T decide)

Did Spencer K and Mother T decide
To be the way they were or could it be
When heaven divvied out ego and pride
These two were watching Oprah on TV?

Why are true saints so few and far between
What holds us back from being really good
If they could make their virtue seem routine
Why don't we do the things we know we should?

And what of evil titans that we know
Who've wrung from living every higher way
And made success embracing what's below
Did they learn sin, or were they born that way?

I think I'm distant from that evil day
But sometimes Spencer seems as far away.

Sonnet 195 (There is the hypothal'mus in the brain)

There is the hypothal'mus in the brain
Which regulates more things than you can tell
Like hunger, sweat, blood pressure, sight and pain
And temperature and body clocks and smell.

It works so automatically profound
You never have to make a choice or think
And though it's silent in the dark background
It knows your every heartbeat, breath and blink.

The body ship would soon be on the rocks
If hypothal'mus took a holiday
A prospect for the undertaker's box
In something like a fraction of a day.

And yet we sometimes live for years and years
Without a useful thought between our ears.

Sonnet 196 (Between my lunch and dinner I was struck)

Between my lunch and dinner I was struck
By passion for a bit of snacking food
And it was, as I foraged, quite my luck
To run across a fruit, still fresh, not stewed.

And thus began my tango with a mango
A luscious lovely dripping ripened thing
That put me in a frenzy and a tangle
To revel in its charming juicy zing.

I smacked and slurped and sucked upon its flesh
And licked my arms and elbows free of drips
And said a prayer of thanks that it was fresh
Then wiped my wrist to clean my sticky lips.

So many distant miles from its tree
This miracle, this mango, feeding me.

Sonnet 197 (A spirit level keeps a project true)

A spirit level keeps a project true
By finding heaven's aspect as a fact
Good builders thus will frequently review
Their vertical and horizontal tact.

A square is also helpful as we build
To keep internal structures lined aright
Without this tool even highly skilled
May see good planning turned into a blight.

The small unmeasured error at the start
Will take us far from course if left unchecked
But if we take these tools to our heart
We'll keep our building true, aligned, correct.

And yet there's those who never get the sense
These tools will build much more than just a fence.

Sonnet 198 (The caravan advanced again today)

The caravan advanced again today
A bit of business fin'lly done up right
As millions met to hear a prophet pray
A scene, once more, of latter day delight.

The ancient and the modern prophets wept
As Spirit with the Father and the Son
Gave proof again that heaven will accept
An offering from persecution won.

And thousands who had been endowed right here
Were felt as unseen witnesses of this
And we joined them in ritualistic cheer
As past and present's perfect reminisce.

Nauvoo redeemed, for good, from evil's grasp
Its temple shining, as it should, at last!

Sonnet 199 (One afternoon in winter I stood still)[viii]

One afternoon in winter I stood still,
Alone, and cold, on empty Parley Street
I watched the temple rising on the hill
And dreamed the details of a great retreat.

I thought I saw the wagons and the stock
And heard the babies cry and teamsters shout
And crowds and line-ups all around the block,
A desperate people, victims of a rout.

Then Parley Street was changed in my mind's eye
To how it was in better days before
As hoards of converts anxiously arrive
To greet a prophet on this hopeful shore.

I didn't come to Parley Street to stay
But part of me will never go away.

Sonnet 200 (I've met this modest man and shook his hand)

I've met this modest man and shook his hand
And heard him bless and laugh and teach and preach
I've marveled at his brilliance and command
Of doctrine, arts, and science and of speech.

I've felt his unassuming love and care
His energy and willingness to lift
I've seen him joined to heaven in a prayer
And work on earth his inexhaustive gift.

I wouldn't rank the prophets if I could
I love them all. God bless each matchless one.
But ask, of all their vision and their good
Which one surpasses what this prophet's done?

Was this his pinnacle at 92
Presiding in the temple, in Nauvoo?

Sonnet 201 (The lonely learn to live that way, and might)

The lonely learn to live that way, and might
At last, be bothered by companionship
Too sensitive to every mood or slight
Annoyed by each remark or jibe or quip.

The feeble find a way to fend as frail
And weak and flimsy fragile sorts, not strong
Instead of changing they may still prevail
By making virtue of what most call wrong.

Few be the ones who change themselves or grow
By adding strength or making friendships more
We tend to change perspective, not the show,
And fail to raise from what we were before.

Far harder to repent and leave our sins
Than redefine our weaknesses as wins.

Sonnet 202 (The hills and mountains rise into the sky)

The hills and mountains rise into the sky
A jagged line as stark as night from day
Dividing earth from heaven, to the eye,
Defining the extent of sunlight's ray.

We think its there on cloudy misty nights
Just hiding from the shame of darkened place
We think it doesn't climb into the heights
Or dip below the dust in dull disgrace.

Illusion that it was before its fall
A mindless misperception of the blue
Horizon isn't really there at all
Unseen or seen, it really can't be true.

Deceived, we make a tool of the lie
Believed, we make a prison of the sky.

Sonnet 203 (The rushing winds of summer's sultry night)

The rushing winds of summer's sultry night
Sly gifts from canyons spilling, spinning, strong
As quick and warm as words provoked by spite
Returning to the depths where they belong.

This pooling place for passing changing lives
A valley floor of gladness and despair
Where cruelty and charity survives
Enjoined by hotter, higher, mountain air.

I have my little lot among the rest
Down here where all that's dear is closely by
My little hiding place, my private nest,
My shelter from the wind, the heat, the sky.

Still every night I'm tested by this breeze
This restless wind that strips away my ease.

Sonnet 204 (We hear of children stolen in the night)

We hear of children stolen in the night
Or even dragged away from play by day
Of parents, in an instant, full of fright,
Of neighbors searching, gathering, to pray.

We see the fam'lies begging on the screen
In hopeless hopefulness and helpless pain
We sort and argue through the clues on scene
We question, but we really can't explain.

Each devil stealer once, himself, was young
A baby in his mother's caring arms
Then innocent, as lullabies were sung,
To bless him with her kindness and her charms.

Which of these tragic mothers' grief is least,
The mother of the victim or the beast?

Sonnet 205 (The men in 1923 wore suits)[ix]

The men in 1923 wore suits
And starched white long sleeved shirts, and solemn ties
They favored vests and shiny blackened boots
And pulled their dark felt hats across their eyes.

They came in buggies, mostly, in the heat
Each wife, beside, in skirts extremely wide,
And in the back, behind their parents' seat,
Small children, all awonder with this ride.

A day of promise binding yesterday
To everafter, everlasting love
And fixing new importance to the way
Between their struggles here, and what's above.

In just one day in 1923
These fam'lies blessed for all eternity.

Sonnet 206 (My self portrait is boldly done and bright)

My self portrait is boldly done and bright
I chose a heavy brush and colors strong
I filled the empty canvas first with light
Then added brilliant strokes both wide and long.

I did the bones before I made the flesh
The muscles had to have a place to hold
A frame so sturdy, powerful and fresh
My history demanding to be told.

But hiding all of this is shadow skin
Transparent? Almost. False? Perhaps, and pale
Here subtlety and subterfuge begin
Here even careful observations fail.

But trouble not about this outward guise
I'll paint a window for you, in my eyes.

Sonnet 207 (Perhaps we've heard the last of Traficant)

Perhaps we've heard the last of Traficant
That stumbling bumbling serpent with a rug
That good ole boy, the master of the rant,
That imp, curmudgeon, congressman and thug.

He beat a bribery rap to make his name
And never learned the evils of his ways
He came, and stayed, and left the House, in shame
The first and only one to shout his praise.

The vote to sack him: Yea's were 4-2-0,
The Nay's just one; and rather famous too!
A Congressman we all have come to know
As one that intern Chandra Levy knew.

You couldn't make this story up, why try?
The truth is always stranger than a lie.

Sonnet 208 (A footprint tells us things we want to know)[x]

A footprint tells us things we want to know
A track that's either new or growing old
It could be found in mud, or dust or snow
A trail that's sometimes faint or brave and bold.

It tells who has been by and hints of when,
Reveals the size and speaks of gait and pace
And captures things forgotten now and then
A snapshot of another time and place.

And while we read these clues in soil and sand
Of those who've passed along this way before
The secrets left in heart or mind or hand
Outweigh the worth of any woodland lore.

I wish I had the priceless skill and art
To leave but cherished traces in the heart.

Sonnet 209 (Why doesn't anybody ever cast)

Why doesn't anybody ever cast
A string or two of pearls, bright and big,
With sparkle and a value unsurpassed
Before the wretched poor pathetic pig?

And why don't people of a certain ilk
Make mention of a donkey or a cow
Instead of when they want a purse of silk
They mock the silly sorry simple sow?

The porcine population has it tough
Synonymous with "filthy", "stinky", "fat"
A reputation worse than Puss or Ruff
Though not as bad as spider, snake or rat.

Still ev'ry swine's best PR is a fork
Connected to some "bacon", "ham" or "pork".

Sonnet 210 (In battles 'gainst a world of fiends and foes)

In battles 'gainst a world of fiends and foes
The boxer in the ring stands all alone
He, only, takes the insults and the blows
And feels the pain to heart and flesh and bone.

Most warriors need a corner for respite
With anxious, helping, cornermen on call
To study how he's doing in the fight
And make a plan to help him win the brawl.

To strategy they add their earnest cheers
And fan his face and forehead with a towel
They build him up against his doubts and fears
Then mend his cuts and wipe his sweaty brow.

With cornermen too zealous or too slack
Some boxers have to fight AND watch their back.

Sonnet 211 (Now scattered, worn and lost, from form of old)

Now scattered, worn and lost, from form of old
Each sacred stone unsanctified in part,
Eroded day and night by heat and cold
As broken as a tattered bleeding heart.

Scant trace of blessed mortar can be found
As weather's wind and water deconstruct
A promise, once inviolate, now unbound
A tender blossom prematurely plucked.

Yet that same ancient builder builds anew!
And holy walls of wonder raised afresh
Give of the maker testament and true
That sacred stony temples clothe his flesh.

And best of all! The promise that no frost
Can breach these walls replacing those once lost.

Sonnet 212 (The way that water plays its games is great)

The way that water plays its games is great
In clouds, in lakes, in snow or glacier fields
It can be vapour or be condensate
Or mist or steam or what a fog bank yields.

A bev'rage or a bath or wash for cars
A sure fire way to put a sure fire out
A soaking place for peaches in their jars
A crowd controlling cannon with a spout.

It's fun, sometimes, to play at getting wet
To splash and dive and kick and swish and swim
Or use a sinker, hook and line and net
Or fill a simple glass beyond the brim.

And don't forget the miracle on ice!
Yes water really does make living nice.

Sonnet 213 (The tiny trees were lonely, wide apart)

The tiny trees were lonely, wide apart
Just reaching to a careless toddler's chest
Three infant trees, a modest sylvan start
Each far too small to harbor any nest.

It took a decade for the trees to make
The rank of roots that never mind the dry
And set to sending limbs that seemed to take
A grasping greedy portion of the sky.

Another decade, and the three had grown
Almost together, and to such an height,
That high and wide, and like a giant throne,
They formed a solid curtain 'gainst the light.

And so, to find the missing morning sun
A former toddler felled the biggest one.

Sonnet 214 (This house was built with Tylenol and tears)

This house was built with Tylenol and tears
The tattered roof is tiles of thin neglect
The floors are covered thick with ancient fears
The windows, crystal glass, that just reflect.

This house is on a sidehill, in the shade
Its gate is hidden from the public road
Its purpose lost, if not, in faith, betrayed
Its essence indecipherable code.

There are no other houses near this one
Alone, it stands, and lost, as if a ghost
A symbol of great hopes, now all undone
A structure false to what it seemed to host.

This house, this husk, this shadow of a soul
Awaits a savior's pledge to be made whole.

Sonnet 215 (Fierce like a Samurai to slice to bone)

Fierce like a Samurai to slice to bone
Her eyes as dark as cloudy moonless nights
Unkind as steel and cold as winter stone
Embodiment of all that uninvites.

Betraying nothing but resolve to spoil
The feeble claims of advocates to grace
To everything that's kind and good, the foil,
This warrior's windowless and distant face.

Tis vain to judge by icy countenance,
A brandished iron arm may hide a heart
So tender in it's armored crust that once
Exposed it would be, ever, torn apart.

Still, threatened by this grim and shadowed shell
One tends to trust the heart is hard as well.

Sonnet 216 (We think that falling water heals the soul)

We think that falling water heals the soul.
The way it mixes light with constant change
So textured, living, pure and colorful
It sings in ev'ry pitch, with endless range.

Why does it dance so deep into the heart
And draw us nigh to it from 'cross the earth,
What makes us feel as if... Right from the start
This splashing's but a shadow of our birth?

Perhaps you've passed a waterfall and not
Been nourished by its glory or its grace
Or trudging, grudging, you have passed it, fought
Desire to kneel in awe before its face.

We look to falling water to be cured
And find some things unseen, but still assured.

Sonnet 217 (Who comforts soldiers adds a weight to war)

Who comforts soldiers adds a weight to war
And sets himself against the soldiers' foes
And while most battles end in frightful gore
The outcome may depend on gentler blows.

Tis treason to give aid to enemies
To feed or offer balm of any sort
Assist, or arm or even to appease
To give the slightest gesture of support.

Yet it is written that we ought to pray
And do some good for those who wish us ill
It puts disciples in an awful way
To study war and still that rule fulfill.

And if your neighbor be defined as all
How does one honor war and heed this call?

Sonnet 218 ("Why don't you join us?" sings the siren maid)

"Why don't you join us?" sings the siren maid
Her invitation warm as hothouse air
Dispelling, in an instant, cruel shade,
A call to come together. Gather. Share.

I turn my back upon the dismal night
My face a new and brilliant summer moon
Quite tempted by her welcome sunny light
Excited by her modest, kindly tune.

I hesitate, and wonder. If I come,
How could I ever bear to have to leave
And go back to the shadows I've come from
And add this loss to everything I grieve?

It tests my faith to welcome every dawn
When every night the siren's call's withdrawn.

Sonnet 244 The Daze that Whine Exposes

You know that high pitched noise as modems shake
their virtual hands in telephone embrace
that starts the interactive give and take
we call a dialogue in cyberspace.

At first we loved this electronic sound,
this miracle, this synapse of hardwires,
and smiled at its bounce, and then rebound,
fulfillment of our Internet desires.

But soon connections seemed to take too long
and since our wishes overshadow need
and knowing that phone links are never strong
we found ourselves in envy of high-speed.

And so, with cable, we've expelled the whine,
of modems shaking hands on our phone line.

Sonnet 252   "For Bertha"

She knows something of want, of war, and nights
Alone. And widowed days too still for ease
Of losing, one by one, life's fatal fights
And how old age reduces by degrees.

The weary loss of youthful flights of song
The struggle to guard memories grown cold
The weight of what was once, but now is gone.
The daily petty thefts of growing old.

And yet, against this ever rising tide
Her countenance and character beguile
She's kept her faith, her confidence, her pride
Her grace, her warmth, her humour and her smile.

And though she from our neighbourhood departs
We'll keep her love and courage in our hearts.

2003

Sonnet 259 - To give acclaim to self I see as pride

To give acclaim to self I see as pride
Unseemly, untoward, and low of heart
A sin, a fault, a character divide
A sign of siding with my smaller part.

And so I would not laud my face or hand
Or give applause to what my fingers do
Or celebrate my voice as something grand
Or dare declare as best my point of view.

And yet to praise the one who's just as near
Who is my bone of bones and flesh of flesh
I do, without regret, excuse or fear.
Extol, and honour, venerate and bless.

The breath, the love, the beauty of my life.
My friend. My soul. My confidant. My wife!

Sonnet 273 The trail of time is marked by diverse threads

The trail of time is marked by diverse threads
Fresh woven into life and ever then
Behind, as record of our passage spreads
A tapestry of everywhere we've been.

Some golden, pure and bright, may decorate
Some steely, strong and hard, may hold the weave
Some wide, unbridled, broad, accelerate
And some, not what we thought they were, deceive.

Each moment weaves its strands into the days
And patterns over years become defined
And everyone will choose which yarn he plays
And leave an honest record, intertwined.

If each be but a weaver. Slave or king.
The choice of fibers, then, is everything.

Sonnet 287 Disabled by the Owner of the List

"Disabled by the owner of the list"
Cast out without a warning by the host
It does no good to shake my little fist
I don't exist because I cannot post.

If summer wasn't coming I might dread
The ostracism offered by this fate
But sunshine offers such a better thread
I'll play outside instead of "e" debate.

And when this summer goes into retreat
And indoor fun comes back into the fore
I hope to find a place more indiscreet
That won't discriminate against this bore.

A list without intelligence or wit
The sort of place where folks like me might fit.

Sonnet 288 I Find the Taste of Spam a Little Off

I find the taste of Spam a little off
Not sharp or fine or mellow or delish
To food, it's like a fever is to cough
A sign of something evil in your dish.

But poor as Spam can be, (and it's real bad!)
It should not be compared to email slop
That unrelenting imposition had
Upon those powerless to make it stop.

And so the inbox of the innocent
Is stuffed with smut and seamy huckster's wares
That bring their putrid rotten email scent
To stink our bandwidth like ripe sewer airs.

I 'spect there'll be a special spot in hell
For those who send unwanted noxious mail.

Sonnet 289 At least I have my spam to keep me warm

At least I have my spam to keep me warm
To savor in the quiet times of day
To entertain, entice, and ..., well, to charm
To turn my working day from toil to play.

It's nice to know I could buy tiny cams
To peek in every room I need to see
Or earn a lot of cash by sending spams
To every email address there could be.

Or that I could be losing lots of weight
Or earn a law degree without the sweat
Or find a former friend, an old class mate,
Or borrow cash to get me out of debt.

But best all, far better than their ware
The volume of their mail is proof they care.

Sonnet 290 Fifty Reasons Not to Write Poems

Misunderstood, ignored, confused and mocked
Perplexed, bemused, belittled, overwrought
Surprised, mistaken, lost and mildly shocked
Dismissed, dismayed, displeased, dissuade, distraught.

Exposed, at risk, alone, unsafe, quite bare
Critique, breakdown, analysis, review
Uncalled, unjust, unwarranted, unfair
Depressed, discouraged, taunted, all askew.

Rebuffed, forgot, denied, gainsaid, left out
Befuddled mystified and bamboozled
A sulk, a wink, a nod, a silly pout
Cajoled, consoled, untold, it all gets old.

And I could give a hundred reasons more
Most people don't write poems anymore.

Sonnet 291 Take Pleasure in the Triumphs of the Rest

Take pleasure in the triumphs of the rest
Too soon your own may fade and pass away
If life for you embraces all that's best
You must delight in every sunny day.

The jealous heart is always sharply sore
For someone somewhere 's always better off
And envy's never able to ignore
The slightest good betrayed by spiteful scoff.

And so if others have the rain you want
Or bask in sun while zephyrs chill your spine
It's better if you hold your wish to taunt
And don't allow yourself to cry or whine.

And then if nothing ever goes your way
At least you can enjoy MY sunny day.

2004

Sonnet 299 The Lambs

The flock is thinning out in Iowa
That caucus mumbo-jumbo did its thing
And all these machinations proved the law
That unintended consequences bring.

He hadn't ought to lose this way. Poor Dick.
Assassinated by his very own
And what's with Howard? Up till now so slick
That upward slope he climbed so long turned down.

And these two Johns who so seduced the state
What corn fed beefs engaged their delegates?
How will the battle turn when Wesley's fate
And gentle Joe's is joined when Hampshire rates?

The lambs are fewer now, not far to go
And soon the sacrificial lamb we'll know.

Sonnet 306 The Snow

This snow, this mystery of light and cold
Disgruntled slave to wind, and sun, and fire
Its maiden dance so terrible and bold
An icy blanket bent to hide desire.

All secret underneath its swollen drifts
As diamond coursing through a prismed lens
Will blind the very eyes it lights and lifts
Its jealousy relentlessly attends.

Some snow will last a thousand unmarked years
And never know the cruel warmth of spring
And thus, be never changed from snow to tears
Or feel the metamorphis seasons bring.

But where I beat my lonely ragged track
I know the sun will win the meadow back.

Sonnet 307 Renewal

Renewal comes at such a heavy price
As winter claims the last of autumn's prize
And while the snow looks wonderful and nice
It hides that deathly business from my eyes.

And even as I slog along this breast
Of freshly fallen powdered crystal snow
My tracks attract attention from the rest
Of nature as it travels to and fro.

The tell tale signs of life and death emerge
Along my beaten path on meadow deep
And study of it makes my own blood surge
As fear within me starts its awful creep.

And all the signs I'm seeing seem to say
There is real danger in this snowy way.

Sonnet 311 Hello, I am a sonnet

Hello, I am a sonnet, how are you?
My principles full conflicted as such
And so to seek the essence of what's true
I probe about with fumbling poet's touch.

I tell my stories openly and sure
Though kindness is my watchword and my goal
Intentions, though uncompromised and pure
Confuse my little part of nature's whole.

You'll find me dancing, yearning, fighting... hard
To tear away the crust of lost desires
To overturn the gambler's hidden card
Exposing acrobats as cheats and liars.

Hello, I am a sonnet, how are you?
Too bad the half of what I tell's untrue

Sonnet 318 Scant Scansion

We see them playing tennis without nets
Absorbed in metaphysics without rules
Not honouring the points, or games, or sets
And calling those who do a bunch of fools.

They hoot it from their great and spacious place
Apocalyptic harbingers these saints
So wrapped up in their intimate embrace
That every prophet's word evokes complaints.

They dance to any drumbeat that they hear
Discipleship? Anathema! Harsh controls.
No notion is invalid! That's their cheer
And iron rod reliance chills their souls.

Analysis without a form at all.
Scant scansion is the sign of their downfall.

Sonnet 320 There's someone somewhere has that dream of mine

There's someone somewhere has that dream of mine
They've got it, paid for, totally in hand
They're past the need to add to or refine
To polish, extend, broaden or expand.

Their talent or increase is o'er the brim
They overflow with what it is I lack
And where my bag of gatherings hangs thin
It spills, it splits, it overwhelms their sack.

I should find comfort in my smaller share
Allowing some are lesser blessed than I
But it's a sin to covet or compare
So patience is the virtue that I'll try.

It's Monday morning somewhere – coming light
But where I am it's only Sunday night.

Sonnet 342 Proverbs 31: 10

What is so great about this claim for good
Why worry if she's virtuous or not
Must worthiness be key to womanhood
And every woman's life be without spot?

The duty to preserve morality
Must rest with equal weight upon the man
And female virtue, in reality
Can only bear its sway on half the plan.

Still, if she's righteous, clean and modest too
She will be saving more than her own fate
More precious than mere rubies to be true
Her virtue will keep other sinners straight.

I see some women falling, failing, low
Cheap Rubies. Costume jewelry for show.

Sonnet 360 One comes to Christ in love or not at all

One comes to Christ in love or not at all
And feels the sweet embracing peaceful touch
The calm, the debt, the worship and the call
Once lame, now free of fear or any crutch.

One finds in Christ acceptance and true grace
The all encompassing, immersing, flood
Pure charity and mercy in one face
Redemption offered freely, bought by blood.

One joins with Christ to share, to warn, to serve
An offering of will, of work, of mind
A fellow with the rest who don't deserve
Heart willing to be knit with all mankind.

And yet He has detractors, not a few
And you're not with Him 'til they hate you too.

Sonnet 362 Good Morning

A six egg omelet overdone by half
The shallots crisp in butter from the start
And cheddar extra old was for the laugh
While swiss on top was there to warm my heart.

I garnished it with vine riped little toms
And sat down at the Internet to eat
To see if there were any new made psalms
Been posted as an early morning treat.

But no, just what I'd done myself, last night
That little sonnet about "going to"
And so I quickly ate my egg delight
And chewed on how I might myself renew.

I hope today I'm worthy of the trust
That God imparts upon the good and just.

Sonnet 367 Lighten up, no really! Lighten up.

Don't give me all this talk of dirty panes
Or slugs or slime or even escargot
Don't be the one who recklessly complains
Of thoughts like this: let's make an embargo!

Instead, get in your SUV my friend
And drive it far above the beaten road
Then count the stars, until the night time's end
Cause every dawn's a gift of hope bestowed.

The black, the dark, the low, the cold, the gray
Evaporate and dissipate and die
And born again is light and faith each day
As we look up into the morning sky.

The sun will lead you, tenderly and true
If you will let him get inside of you.

2005

Sonnet 389 Entangled (D&C 43:9, 82:10, & 88:86)

The devil likes to tangle up his prey
To tie you up with fiery flaxen cords
His bindings growing tighter every day
Each sin cinched up by its prescribed rewards.

The Lord has granted freedom by decree
But asks that you pledge freely to obey
And states the consequence "will bind up Me!
No promise" if you don't do what I say.

These two enticers vying for your soul
The auction underway and going strong
The rope entirely in your control
The choice is clear. It's either right. Or wrong.

So there you go, decide which knot to do.
Will God be bound, or will your sins tie you.

Sonnet 391 The things I did on Saturday

I swept the sawdust up and fixed some lines
to bring the cabled world to my lair
I rode my bike between majestic pines
and cut the bit that passes for my hair

I took three trips to buy some dark grey paint
and sprayed it on the old retaining wall
I spent my evening gathered as a saint
and shopped for groceries at the local mall.

I watched a hurricane flood evermore
and guaranteed a passport for a friend
I fed the cats and helped them through the door
then went to bed to signal this day's end.

The sum of all this simple mundane lot
is what will make a worthy life... or not.

Sonnet 392 I should have read a thousand books by now

I should have read a thousand books by now
The most, unblessed stories of the days
And nights of countless pilgrims learning how
To cross the wilderness of human ways.

Each Adam seeking happiness or yet
Just reconciling life and pain and death
Sometimes with artfulness so great is met
Descriptions of the joy of drawing breath.

Still most were less than that and left me wrecked
No wiser for the journey through their leaves
But one, the best of all, was most correct
A perfect test against a world deceived.

And reading it just once again before
Is better than to read a thousand more.

Sonnet 393 He worships at the altar of his choice

He worships at the altar of his choice
Devoted to the flavor of the day
His practice is to study and rejoice
Then shift to something else along the way.

She firmly keeps her faith in just one thing
As rigid as self righteousness can be
Her flights, attempted on that single wing,
Don't ever rise above her bended knee.

I'm searching for some kind of higher ground
I'm sorting through the dross for gold to keep
Embracing and rejecting things I've found
Determined to continue 'til I sleep.

The truth's too precious to be cast aside
And far too large to be confined by pride.

Sonnet 393

The gravity of many things we know
In pounds and ounces, grams and measures such
The weightiness of matter we can we show
By math, not just a little or too much

Still some things press upon us we can't weigh
Those matters that don't measure on the scales
The balance, rather, upon which they play
Will shift as faith or hopelessness prevails.

And some will count it worse to have to wait
The agony of "if" they've won or lost
Unknowing is for them the worst of fate
And so they beg to know at any cost.

But hope is such a light and airy thing
It leavens any burden life can bring.

Sonnet 395 The innocent is tempted thus to dance

Thin edge, slight slip, forbidden furtive glance
Enticements ever beckoning the soul
The innocent is tempted thus to dance
Beyond permitted edges of control.

The flaxen cord lies limp and ever near
At ready for the smallest vaguest chance
To coil in a knot of gentle fear
And make its deadly threatening advance.

Turn back, pull out, retreat, repent, just leave!
Before the cart rope grows into a chain
And gathers all the strength that hell can weave
From sins played once, replayed, then played again

The noose is patient merciless and sure
The devil's final irreparable cure.

2006

Sonnet 397 To probe a wound or find a fallen coin

To probe a wound or find a fallen coin
To see into the depths of any haze
These tasks demand the searcher gladly join
His eye with light to set the scene ablaze.

Some think that serious reasoning is best
When driven by the engine of pure doubt
That criticism makes a worthy test
And questioning is what it's all about.

While others want to be indentured friends
Disciples, full of hope and love and trust
Believers of beginnings and of ends
For them it's faith that constitutes the must.

They can't see how enlightenment can come
From casting shadows where the hunting's done.

Sonnet 398 I like to keep an empty shelf or two

I like to keep an empty shelf or two
A place inviting, open, free and spare
A contrast to the clutter in my view
That every other cupboard seems to bear.

Why don't I simply organize the whole
And make them each and all a tidy sight
The composite in harmony's control
Instead of barren contrasting with blight?

My empty offering to average out
May only highlight more the troubled part
But in my view of it the shelves without
Atone some way for flaws that grip my heart.

Still, heaven wouldn't tolerate such pranks
To try to neutralize your sins with blanks!

Sonnet 403 Another High Council Meeting Goes Until After 11

The yawning starts in earnest about ten
Til then it's just the early risers who
Are struggling to maintain a useful ken
Against this time that fills the mind with glue.

And so I sit and wonder what to do
My instinct tells me "Set us free right now!"
And struggles to defeat, deny, subdue
The promptings to instruct - to teach - somehow.

And usually I resist the call to quit
And offer something as a parting thought
And thereby add more yawning with my bit
As it gets ever later as we're taught.

But then, at least, I hope, that adds some fun
To all the work this sleepy bunch has done.

2007

Sonnet 404 A Day Without a Poem

A day without a poem is surely lost
and barely worth the breath it took to keep
the fire burning at such awful cost
when nothing was produced but smoke and heat.

A picture might be called a poem I guess
a kiss, a hug, a tender word, a wink
recordings which in mind and heart impress
and make a subtle lifelong bond or link.

Still better to be written on a page
to save against forgetfulness or loss
preserved from now for any future age
impressions, visions, intuition's toss.

A poem unread, unlike a scorned embrace
will offer to the wind some hopeful trace.

Sonnet 405 Routine has wrestled writing to the ground

An after Christmas lull has hit my muse.
Routine has wrestled writing to the ground
The most of me, it seems, is fully used
By gravity in daily chores I've found.

But then, I think the holidays were much
The same or so it seemed, that life was rife
And everything was new and out of touch
And left with no more time to share my life.

I guess my muse will come and go in spurts
There's no accounting for when it will rise
Or fall, in intermittent floods or squirts
Consistency will be in the surprise!

How much like other parts of life is this?
Some disappointment sprinkled with some bliss.

Sonnet 406 Rolling Coins

The quarter or some coin that likes to glide
Is pinched by Thumb and Pointer as annex
Then pushed on top of Pointer on a slide
That trips it in the space against Index.

And so it rolls and lands, a happy fling
And deftly Pointer pushes til it meets
Across the top of Index down by Ring
And whereupon again the flip repeats.

Now Pinky's where the rolling coin ends
And Thumb must catch it quick and slide it back
Along the bottom of its three long friends
Until it's pushed once more above on track.

I love to feel my knuckles make coins dance
Just one of many things I learned in France.

2008

Sonnet 468 Rose Pedals[xi]

If dropping roses from the canyon heights
And listening for echoes from the walls
Could give a man the courage of his rights
I'd toss a pedal to each heart that calls.

There's people out there I have never met
Much more, in fact, than I can call my friends
And quite a few, I think if I could get
To know, would grow from what a rose extends.

And so I lift myself from that plain dread
That slams against my better nature's will
And cast, with roses, hopefully some bread
Upon the water deep below this hill.

If no one else is lifted, blessed or fed
At least my wounds are stitched with my own thread.

Sonnet 469 Renew

Recharge, renew, reclaim, refresh, revive
It sometimes takes retreat to do these things
The trauma of a constant forward drive
May use up all the fuel in our wings.

The muse may not be lost as we suspect
But merely taking nourishment from rest
To rise again and capture what was checked
And conquer words afresh and newly dressed.

Still, settled back and pondering and slack
The will to battle forth can dull and die
And satisfied by such a peaceful lack
It's hard to mount anew the battle cry.

So does this mean I'm moving out ahead
Or merely rolling over in my bed?

Sonnet 470 Some Contests in the Public Eye Give Shame

Some contests in the public eye give shame
To those who follow, blow by blow, the brawl
Diminishing the audience's name
As well as proving each contestant small.

Still other struggles bring a better fame
To both the fighters and their loyal fans
And where the prize is worthy of the claim
There's honor and there's glory in their plans.

We don't do well in sorting out these things
So often do we cheer for empty wins
And wonder why the victory it brings
Is hollow like the pleasure of our sins.

I wish to never back another fight
Unless to win is honest, true, and right.

Sonnet 471 I Stand in Praise of Metaphor

I stand in praise of metaphor and such
Of parables and fables and of tales
That give of common stories so so much
To ponder in their curious details.

I laud the need to closely read the text
And wonder at why every chosen word
Was placed in order, first or last or next
And which of every meaning is preferred.

I cheer at sorting fiction from the fact
At likening the fable to our ways
At realizing how we interact
With types and shadows from some other days.

I try to mine from every simple story
The allegory's everlasting glory.

Sonnet 472 The Drudge Report Refreshes

The Drudge Report refreshes hour by hour
No news is ever posted there to stay
And CNN is known to devour
A multitude of stories in a day.

It's good for them that we demand no meat
If nothing of import is on the scene
We're satisfied with trivia to eat
We take our news as junk food, not cuisine.

No harm is done, I guess, if we still dine
At better places for a solid meal
And never let the media define
What nourishment is good, or best, or real.

To save from overdose of headline blasts
It may require a course of frequent fasts.

Sonnet 484

I say that no kind deed is ever lost
Although some fall on barren salted ground
And must instead of blessings count a cost
Against the one whose gratitude's unfound.

But most will find a way to penetrate
The hearts and minds of those so kindly blest
To soften and relieve a pris'ner's fate
And brace against the shocks of each day's test.

Those tender words you bravely, kindly send
Or even simple smiles or waves or nods
That recognize another as a friend
Add strength to you, to them, and to the gods.

The greatest sin is to withhold or spare
The grace that God has given you to share.

2009

Sonnet 489 Reflections of Helaman 5:12

There is no place on earth to build that's right
To beat the power of wind and wave and storm
No mix of manmade concrete has the might
To save against what nature can perform.

And even sun and water wear out stone
And granite mountains wash away at last
This world cannot be permanency prone
With so much vigor in destructive blast.

And molten white hot lava at the core
Unstable as the water in the foam
That beats against the ocean's ragged shore
Is threat'ning any time to melt this home.

Don't build your dreams upon this earthy tent
Foundations that endure are heaven sent.

Sonnet 490 Reflections on D&C 76: 22-24

The voice I've heard is not the voice of man
But such as only heart and soul can feel
Yet stronger and more true than any plan
Devised to prove that something else is real.

And so because of this I know it's true
The testimony of this Joseph Smith
A declaration meant to best renew
The faith that Christ is not some ancient myth.

And since, the witnesses have multiplied
Until in millions saints affirm the Christ
And though they each have truly testified
Still, for the rest, it does not yet suffice.

Each must just ask to hear from Him that gives
The voice, at last, that testifies: He lives!

Sonnet 491 Reflections on Proverbs 3: 5-8[xii]

The natural man, and I mean "he", not "she"
Is loath to seek directions on his way
Although he may find map reading a key
His instinct is to try each path in play.

And preference for going his own way
To even being on the better track
Can set into his nature day by day
Until he's lost all want for coming back.

And since he now has not the will to say
In truth and love to God, "Thy will be done"
Then God will sadly say to him some day
In truth and love,"Thy will be done, my son."

Oh grant me strength to ask, to plead to know
The path for me that God would gladly show.

Sonnet 492 Reflections on D&C 121: 45-46

You've got to feel the love deep in yer gut
The love fer all yer kin and all mankind
And keep yer thoughts all clear of any smut
In simplest terms that's gospel truth defined.

And yet it ain't so simple, not a bit
To love, in fullness and across the board
Requires a change of heart that just won't quit
And purity of mind that can't be scored.

It's like all theories 'splained by just one graph
There's too much mystery in this little verse
Just thinkin bout it busts my brain in half
What's more, the more I think, the more its worse.

Don't even try to ponder on the rest -
Rewards fer those who figure out this test.

Sonnet 493 Reflections on Mosiah 3:19

Who wants the artificial anymore?
Promotions of what's natural are bold
Just look around in any grocery store
It's natural that cries out to be sold.

And in our "feels good" value sort of way
We laud the basest instincts of the man
No talk of rising up above that fray
We hunker down, accepting any plan.

But God would have us reach a new plateau
Not artificial, but more real by far
Put off the ordinary and the low
And climb above your nature, to a star.

And how to climb is irony supreme
Put on his easy yoke and find your dream.

Sonnet 494 Reflections on Ephesians 4: 31-32

We easily can see in some the fault
Of being lost in bitterness and wrath
Whose lives are but a clamorous assault
Against a kind and peaceful sort of path.

And such are tragic figures to be sure
Who need repentance and relief a pace
And yet the scripture has a broader cure
Than only those with such complete disgrace.

For we are counseled here to put off all
Our anger and our evil speaking ways
And all, is not a challenge trite or small
A test enough to puzzle and amaze.

O make me tenderhearted through and through
So I'll forgive, and be forgiven too.

Sonnet 495 Reflections on Mosiah 4:30

Some principles have proxies in the writ
Alternative or stand-in words that point
To something more important than the bit
Of meaning that the words themselves anoint.

To show it, here's a test you ought to try
Replace a word with something else and see
If meanings are unlocked when you apply
The proxy to the passage as a key.

Now where you read "remember" say "repent"
Then think if that expands the verse's aim
And next, see if it adds to what is meant
If you give "watch yourselves" the same new name.

First principles are rife with proxy friends
The scripture student's magnifying lens.

Sonnet 496 Reflections on 2 Timothy 1:7-8

Each time we take the sacrament we pledge
Three things: His name. Remember. And command
And if we keep these covenants our edge
Will be to have his Spirit close at hand.

And when we listen to the Spirit's voice
Three things: His Power. Love. And a sound mind
Become the badges of that prudent choice
And should be testified to all mankind.

And yet another spirit gives us fear
And shame to try to keep us from the right
It never deals in matters of good cheer
Nor power. Love. Or wisdom. Just with fright.

If you're afraid to do the things you should
You're listening to the spirit that's not good.

Sonnet 497 Reflections on Alma 34:32

Some think that life was accident'lly won
By chemistry in some primordial soup
And then progressed as evolution done
By mutants growing fitter than their group.

They do not see the hand of God in this
We're only just by chance and then we're gone
And so we slip back into the abyss
Our purpose well fulfilled if we leave spawn.

But prophets tell us life has real intent
That it's a preparation and a test
And that we must be faithful and repent
To earn a grade at judgment that's the best.

And everyone can know that this is true
Just listen to that voice inside of you.

Sonnet 498 Reflections on 1 Nephi 3:7

It can't be fun to do as Nephi did
Oh sure we envy faith like his a lot
But we don't line up for his type of bid
What he is selling isn't often bought.

We buy instead the line that other's sell
The one that says we have to think ahead
And only do what common sense will tell
Be safe, be sure, plan every step you tread.

All Nephi had to work with was his trust
Not knowing in advance the how or when
That God upon declaring what he must
Had done the preparation for his win.

Yeah, that can't be much fun. And stressful too!
I'll stick with doing things the way I do.

Sonnet 499 Reflections on Moses 1:39

That battle that began before this time
Is all about the agency of man
It's not a point that's subtle or sublime
You choose your fate by picking out a plan.

The one is mis'ry all dressed up as fun
The rebel call in irony complete
By disobedience their fates undone
They lose it all by opting for a cheat.

The other is surrender to a way
That works a mighty paradox of love
Your freedom found by learning to obey
A Father who defends you from above.

His work and glory tied to your success
His focus is entirely to bless.

Sonnet 500 Reflections on Moses 7:18

It's hard to even dream of such a place
Where everyone is of one heart and mind
And where there is not even any trace
Of anything unrighteous or unkind.

And more that even that I find it hard
To fathom life without the poor around
No weak, no foolish, and no lame or scarred
No low, no slow, no simple and no clown.

No hungry and no hostages of fate
No puny or pathetic hanging back
No beggars and no blind to contemplate
No lazy with their lives all out of whack.

And where do you suppose that you will be
When Zion is declared to be poor-free?

Sonnet 501 Reflections on Mosiah 5:15

The choice we think is between being strong
And being human and, of course, then weak
And while we don't enjoy being wrong
We nurture this as if it meant we're meek.

But really, everyone is constant and steadfast
We seldom waiver in the things we clasp
Our grip is always strong enough to last
It's all about what things we choose to grasp.

The sinner may be faithful to his sin
Immovable as any saint can be
It's clear his choice of what to hold won't win
And yet he clings to it so steadfastly!

In fact addiction therapy is there
For those who so abound in their despair.

Sonnet 502 Reflections on 2 Nephi 12:3

A joke with heavy wisdom is the one
Where someone says "You can't get there from here."
And also do we sometimes just for fun
Select a road "least travelled by" that's clear.

And think about the saying wise and smart
That says that any road at all will do
To satisfy your undecided heart
If you don't know just where you're going to.

Come to the mountain of the Lord and ask
If it be true that all roads lead to Rome
Or must a certain strait and narrow path
Be chosen for a child to get back home.

And can we have all that the Father hath
If we don't learn to walk his given path?

Sonnet 503 Reflections on Malachi 4: 5-6

We know this scripture means to turn your heart
To those who died before they got the chance
In life to share in the great gospel part
That's needed to eternally advance.

And some are expert at researching lines
And others get to temples quite a lot
And some do family scrap booking designs
While others helped the people that they taught.

But even for the ones who don't do such
Who never get their generations found
They honour the intent almost as much
By turning heart to family that's around.

We save from many curses when we strive
To turn our hearts to family that's alive.

Sonnet 504 Reflections on D&C 88: 119

Wonderful, Counselor, the Mighty King
The Everlasting Father, Prince of Peace
These words don't speak, or call or shout: They sing!
T'was Handel's music gave them such increase.

And we need a Handel writing in our time
To make this verse a temple anthem true
To drive into our hearts like holy rhyme
These preparation principles anew.

Oh sure we have our sacred Hymn by Phelps
But it is not so faithful to the writ
For what we need is something more that helps
Both spirit and the actual words commit.

Musicians of the kingdom please endow
These sacred words with fitting music now.

Sonnet 505 Reflections on Matthew 11: 28-30

The yoke has been a genius way to pack
As long as any cargo has been hauled
You cannot share the power of legs and back
Unless some sort of harness is installed.

And best to be yoked up with someone strong
Enough to lighten any sort of weight
Someone whose help is never slight or wrong
Who offers peace and rest without debate.

And burdens much more grave than gravity
Like sin and loss and grief and death and pain
Are carried in that endless cavity
That such a yoke can lift without a strain.

Why heap your burdens in a careless pile
When He would help you carry them in style?

Sonnet 506 Reflections on 2 Nephi 25:26

We sometimes play a game of hide and seek
Or scavenge hunt for objects just for fun
Or share the secrets of Nimrod's technique
In deer camp while we polish up our gun.

Also we tease our children to pursue
Things lost. To learn the joy of what's found.
And have the faith and confidence anew
To search for truth where counterfeits abound.

But do not be deceived or fail to note
Your child will sometime feel he's lost... depressed
His sin will bring eternal loss of hope
Unless he knows the source of peace and rest.

So if your children will avoid torment
They must be taught, by you, how to repent.

Sonnet 507 Reflections on Leviticus 19:18

It's fun to eat a piece of chocolate fudge
But nothing's fun about a bitter grudge
And no one likes their work to have a smudge
But it's still worse to hold an angry grudge.

And I would rather ride than have to trudge
But even worse would be to bear a grudge
And no one likes a biased unfair judge
The kind, I guess, who holds some sort of grudge.

And who has not been bogged in sticky sludge
A fitting metaphor for mired in grudge
And of the headlines featured by Matt Drudge
The worst are those that evidence a grudge.

And foolish stubborn folks will never budge
They cling like monkeys to their every grudge.

Sonnet 508 Reflections on Moroni 10:4-5

When baking something wonderful and sweet
Like bread or cake or pie or quiche or tart
The recipe for such a pleasant treat
Requires attention to its every part.

You won't get far if features are left out
(A bread without its leavening won't rise)
And so the baker wisely is devout
To every step the recipe applies.

And recipes for following truth's way
Must be a code worth more than any bread
And more important therefore to obey
The rules that lead to such a golden thread.

So ponder each instruction in this verse
The most important recipe on earth.

Sonnet 509 Reflections on John 17:3

It's all in who you know, they sometimes say
In pointing out this commonest of trends
For those who hand out favours have a way
Of serving first the needs of their best friends.

And even God insists that you know him
And Jesus Christ, begotten only son
And this is no negotiable whim
Without it your eternity's undone.

And such a deal might seem a bit unfair
To those who find no joy in knowing God
But since his invitation is to share
The justice of the choice is no façade.

The tender mercy of the Prince of love
Will freely lift each willing friend above.

Sonnet 510 Reflections on Ephesians 5: 1,20

I might be thankful for that and for this
For blessings of good fortune and of wealth
For friends and kin and for my marriage bliss
And love and peace and comfort and good health.

And even trouble, to my earthly eyes
Is sometimes plainly for my lasting good
As lessons learned in pain become a prize
That's sweet because it's better understood.

And yet we often cannot see the why
Or slightest reason in this mortal day
For certain things that may afflict and try
And seem to leave no trace of wisdom's way.

Yet if by giving thanks our faith is tried
The value of the test can't be denied.

Sonnet 511 Reflections on Psalm 100: 1-2

We have so many choices that are tough
The kind that trouble, torment and perplex
It leaves no time to let the easy stuff
Bewilder, puzzle, mystify or vex.

And what could be more simple than this note
To call upon the servants of the Lord
To serve him with that gladness in your throat
That comes out in a song of sweet accord.

So do not hesitate to choose this course
Of making joyful noise in music bright
To celebrate in union with the source
Of life, of happiness and endless light.

Yes other choices may be hard or wrong
But no one should decide against a song.

Sonnet 512 Reflections on John 11: 25-26

So there we have it friends, in just a word
Our fate depends upon belief or not
Yet some of us can even now be heard
To say "We really don't believe a lot".

And that we think belief is not our choice
You either have it or you don't it seems
According to the devil's oily voice
We can't be held accountable for dreams.

And yet, down deep, we know it's right to say
We've weighed the evidence and consequence
And opted for the unbelieving way
Because we didn't like obedience .

Don't fall for Satan's hopeless argument
We can believe. And live! So let's repent!

Sonnet 513 Reflections on Isaiah 53: 4-5

Some words are deep and heavy, wise and strong
With meanings that add feeling to insight
That lift from common prose to lovely song
And generate a special truth and light.

"Grief" and "sorrow", are such weighty terms
And "sticken", "smitten" and "afflicted" too
And "bruised" and "wounded", in a word, confirms
The sacrifice that was atonement's due.

And for us words of equal weight and strength
As we are offered "peace" by what he did
And added to our peace we're "healed" at length
Through his "chastisement" in this awful bid.

It's a good deal for us, by any test
He bears our transgressions and we get blessed.

Sonnet 514 Reflections on 1 Timothy 4:12

The youth himself will sometimes most despise
His opportunity to show belief
Believing that in other people's eyes
His standing is irrelevant and brief.

And so as if humility was his
He carries on unmindful of his chance
To set a good example of what is
In fact, his Christian duty to advance.

And even worse sometimes this grand mistake
Leads to the casual habit of distain
For any actual effort made to shake
Behaviors unacceptable and vain.

So if you want the better path to truth
Become a good example in your youth.

Sonnet 515 Reflections on Amos 3:7

Who doesn't love to learn of secret things
Like truthful treasures, valuable and rare
That's why they market those decoder rings
To those who want both secrets and to share.

And peeping wizards too and magic men
Will make a claim to special powers of sight
By checking out your tea leaves now and then
Or gazing into certain stars by night.

Yet even if these sorceries were true
No value to the information found
Has ever been confirmed upon review
Such secrets being patently unsound.

But God reveals his secrets one by one
To prophets before anything is done.

Sonnet 516 Reflections on Mosiah 7:33

Sometimes some people wallow in their sin
They flounder in their wicked willful lives
Believing that there is no way to win
Redemption from that place where misery thrives.

While others blinded by the path they've strayed
Don't even see their bonds of disbelief.
They do not know or trust of promise made
To those who turn to Christ for sweet relief

So if you lie in chains, yet boast of choice
(Deceived beyond all reason all along)
Or guard your precious bondage with a voice
Of bitter hopeless agony. You're wrong!

From either plight, the lack of faith or sight
There is a path that leads to truth and light.

Sonnet 517 Reflections on D&C 14:7

The poorest parent gives his child some gift
If nothing of this world's goods and strife
Nor even good example as a lift
At least the parent gave the gift of life.

And the Richest and the Best of parents too
May not deliver much of this earth's wealth
But promise in his own due time to do
What's needed for his child's eternal health

And those of us with some of this life's means
Will give from what we have to help our brood
Extending by these tried and true routines
That value of the family we've viewed.

To do better than the poorest, then, I'd guess
That view must be consistent with the Best.

Sonnet 518 Reflections on Moroni 10:32

I wonder when I'm tried for my reward
Will someone testify at that great trial
"Regarding his ungodliness my Lord
The prisoner, I fear, is in denial."

Perhaps before I have to take my turn
Before I reach that final judgment scene
I'd better take the trouble to discern
Just what "deny yourself" might really mean.

For those who don't deny themselves, I see,
From looking closely at this verse of writ
Deny the power of God to some degree
And lose the perfect promises of it.

So what you do and don't deny depends
Upon your choice of your eternal ends.

Endnotes

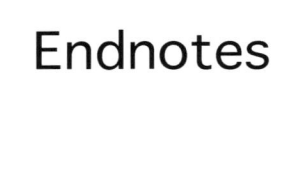

i   Here is the text of the letter that introduced the scripture memorization challenge, and the letter that later modified it. I include it here because it so effectively states my strong feelings about the value of taking the scriptures into our hearts and the blessings that flow from it.

January 4, 2007

Dear Members of the Cardston Alberta Stake,

We have challenged stake members to memorize Helaman 5:12 for December and Doctrine and Covenants 76: 22-24 for January, and we will designate additional scriptures for each of the coming months. We are thrilled and encouraged by the response of so many, of all ages, who have taken up this challenge.

We make a solemn priesthood promise that anyone in the stake suffering from sin, temptation, afflictions, pain, trouble, burdens, or sorrow will be blessed if they will turn to the assigned scripture memorization in the very moment of such temptation or suffering. There will be both strength and solace in the process of committing these words of Christ to memory and then running them through your mind in times of need. They will build in you a greater love for God and his Son and a stronger resolve and increased capacity to build your life upon the Rock of our Redeemer. Study these words, learn them until you have them word perfect, ponder their meanings and the applications of them in your own lives. Repeat them until they flow easily and then continue to repeat them so you don't lose them. This exercise is meant to be an ongoing building process where, at the end of a year, for example, you will know 12 wonderful scripture passages, not that you have learned 12 scriptures and forgotten 10 of them. You will have 12 or more solid comforting, testifying, teaching and edifying passages that are part of your mind, heart and character and available to you at any time to fortify your resistance to temptation, to clear your mind of worrisome or unwholesome thoughts, to turn your thoughts to Christ and His gospel, to help you teach, to lift your spirits, to improve your judgment and to bridle your passions and control your emotions.

Please accept this simple challenge. Some of you have great difficulty memorizing or may be too young or have special circumstances that make extended memorization impossible for you. In those cases please just do as much as you can. Even a very small child could be taught to repeat: "It is upon the Rock of our Redeemer...that you must build your foundation" or "That he lives!" Please adapt this challenge to your individual capacities, but exercise faith and determination and you may be surprised to find capability that you never expected.

In the 5th chapter of John there is described a great healing by the Savior at the waters of Bethesda and the challenge that the Jews made against him for it. He then told them the following:

And the Father himself, which hath sent me, hath borne witness of me. Ye have neither heard his voice at any time,nor seen his shape. **And ye have not his word abiding in you**: *for whom he hath sent, him ye believe not. Search the scriptures; for in them ye think ye have eternal life: and they are they which testify of me.* (John 5:37-39, emphasis added.)

What a tragedy it would be to fail to have "his word abiding" in us. There are many ways, of course, to meet that challenge, but the Savior suggests perhaps the most important and powerful way, and that is to "Search the scriptures". A related response would be to search so thoroughly as to memorize important passages. In a manner of speaking a passage that is embedded in our memory is truly "his word abiding" in us in a most intimate and wonderful way.

May God bless each of us as we go forward searching the scriptures together and memorizing these few selected scriptures and attempting with all sincerity, by thought, word and deed to always have his word abiding in us.
Yours truly,
Stake Presidency

Amendment May 10, 2009
It was announced in Stake Conference that the challenge is now modified. No new scriptures will be added to the thirty presently identified. Each of the scriptures has been numbered according to the order they were assigned and each represents the day of the month corresponding to its number. So the first scripture should be reviewed on the first day of each month, and the second on the second day of each month and so forth. Every day of the month will then have an assigned scripture, and now an assigned hymn as well. Those anxious to continue learning new scriptures are encouraged to make their own choices. Everyone is encouraged to continue to review and ponder these thirty scriptures, and to use them in Family Home Evening, in church

lessons and talks and in daily life.

ii On June 30, 2001 I wrote Sonnet I and now on November 7, 2001, as they say (who are they anyway?) the rest is history. I numbered my first 50 sonnets in Roman Numerals, just like Shakespeare, I thought. And the hardest part about writing 50 sonnets in 4 months or so was dealing with those darned Roman numerals. I had to sit and puzzle it out every time. So I'm swearing off them. Roman numerals, that is. I've gone back and expunged them from my titles.

However, I am hooked on sonnets (as they almost say). That's it, I'm going to publish a volume of my verse and call it "Hooked on Sonnets." I'll bet there would be, oh... maybe V, or VI or maybe even VII people willing to read it. It would come with a guarantee to raise your reading marks by at least I or II letter grades or your money back. (Offer valid only in those places where is cannot be understood or enforced.)

iii   The latest (and only) news headline:
Police: 'Robert Blake shot Bonny Bakley'

iv   Betty and I were blessed to attend a special fireside Sunday night for temple workers. Elder Holland, Elder Hafen and Elder Walker spoke to us. It was very interesting, and one of the impressions that came to me was how seriously the brethren are taking the completion of the Nauvoo temple. Elder Holland shared some of the history of how the plans were miraculously preserved and obtained by the church. And over all it was clear that this marks an important milestone in the restoration. This poem is my own impression and not meant to interpret anything any of the brethren said. Just to remind you. June 27th, the day the dedication sessions begin is also the anniversary of the martyrdom of Joseph Smith "at about 5:00 p.m." (Section 135 of the D&C).

v   " He that is slow to wrath is of great understanding: but he that is hasty of spirit exalteth folly."

vi   "Even a fool, when he holdeth his peace, is counted wise: and he that shutteth his lips is esteemed a man of understanding."

vii   I've watched a couple of nights in the past week as Connie Chung has made her debut on CNN. She seems so uncomfortable and anxious to me that she make me nervous for her. She wants to please too much, to demonstrate wit and insight she doesn't possess. She's like a juggler trying to keep more balls in the air that his skill will permit - the consequence? She drops them all! I hope she recovers soon and tones down and lets the game come to her, or that her public torture is brief. On the other hand.... Larry just rolls along....

viii   It was with a sense of deja vu and amazement that I listened to President Hinckley encourage those at the final dedicatory session tonight to walk down Parley Street and imagine the scene as the pioneers evacuated the city in 1846. I was there in December and spent some of my most profound time along that street. I had to just sit on the shore at the end of the street and look across the water. I think I saw it a lot of different ways.....

ix   The Cardston Alberta Temple was dedicated in 1923.

x   This isn't much of a poem, but the idea for it came out of something interesting. Since the poem doesn't do justice to the idea, I'll lay out the incident that gave me the idea.

Last week I did a little scriptural recitation at a party for all the ordinance workers who work on our particular shift at the temple. Later one of the workers told me that she would never again read or hear that scripture without remembering the testimony that she felt when I recited it. As I pondered this remark I thought about the joy and wonder there is when we are able to leave a mark (for good) in someone's heart. We tromp through life leaving all sorts of marks, but few they be, I suppose, that really matter. Anyway the sonnet isn't a literal representation of the idea, of course, but it does sort of tramp around on that ground.

xi   Wallace Stevens is quoted as saying that publishing poetry is like throwing a rose pedal into the Grand Canyon and listening for the echo.

xii   With apologies to George Macdonald and C.S. Lewis

Manufactured by Amazon.ca
Bolton, ON